EXACTING CLAM No. 8 — Spring 2023

CONTENTS

M000115574

Front cover by Jesi Bender

Interior drawings by Kathleen Nicholls & John Patrick Higgins

ISBN: 978-1-952386-63-3

Exacting Clam is a quarterly publication from Sagging Meniscus.

exactingclam.com

From the Editor

We are grateful to every contributor, every time. In our infancy we have relied on the kindness and enthusiasm of the writers whose work has appeared on these pages. I continue to be astonished at the talent we have somehow attracted. Long may it continue.

As we see out the second year of our existence with this, our eighth issue, I want to offer thanks of a more specific variety.

Firstly, to Jake Goldsmith—not only for his unforgettable contributions to the magazine, but also for his endeavours with The Barbellion Prize, the literary award he founded with a view to promoting work by authors who live with chronic illness or disability. In this issue we take the opportunity to showcase just some of the fine work which has been long- or short-listed for the 2022 prize. With the authors' kind permission, you will read excerpts from Harry Parker's *Hybrid Humans*, Lauren Foley's *Polluted Sex*, Letty McHugh's *Book of Hours: An Almanac for the Seasons of the Soul*, and Polly Atkin's *Recovering Dorothy: The Hidden Life of Dorothy Wordsworth*—works which would grace the list of any literary prize.

Adviser to the prize, Tom Shakespeare, contributes an excerpt from his forthcoming novel, *A Leap in the Dark* (Farrago, 2025). Long-listed author, Dr. Shahd Alshammari, contributes a reflection on her (other) self. Previous winner, Lynn Buckle, is here with a piece on language—but not *that* language.

We're equally delighted that around these Barbellion-specific contributions, a constellation of other work has formed, not directly related to the prize but just the kind of work the prize is intended to encourage. Thrillingly, we have cajoled work out of playwright and poet Dan O'Brien, Exacting Clam illustrator Kathleen Nicholls, writer and composer Matt Tomkinson, former care worker Doug Smith, Exacting Clam contributor Tomoé Hill, New York musician David Holzman and our own Jesi Bender, who contributes an excerpt from her *sui generis* work *Kinderkrankenhaus* (Sagging Meniscus 2021)—on themes as diverse as epilepsy, Crohn's disease, cancer, neurodiversity and mental health.

Thanks to the above, to all the other contributors and to you, for reading. If you would like to support the Barbellion Prize or any of these authors, you know what to do. The prize accepts donations via its home page and I'm sure the authors do too, via book sales. Having familiarized myself with the listed works while preparing this issue, I recommend them all without the slightest hesitation.

— Guillermo Stitch

Letty McHugh

A Miracle Wasted

When I was six years old, I bit off half my nail. I panicked. I didn't want to die. I prayed, then nothing was wrong. A miracle. What if everyone alive only gets one miracle?

I once read about a Monk who fell from Tynemouth Priory three times and survived twice. I bet he wished he'd saved a miracle for that third time he hit the ground. You can imagine how much I wished I hadn't wasted my miracle on a fingernail when I was diagnosed with an incurable illness.

I grew up Catholic. I'm still figuring out what that means to me as an adult. In 1997 it meant I went to Mass on Wednesday's with school and sat wondering why the Corinthians never wrote back to Saint Paul.

I was diagnosed with Multiple Sclerosis in 2012 after I lost feeling in my left leg for a week. I only rang NHS Direct to appease my mother. They said 'Can you make your own way to the hospital? We can send an ambulance', I said 'I'll just ring a taxi.' I was 20, and not really taking anything seriously yet. When I was admitted and my friend had to leave me, I asked her to look up the patron saint of legs. I didn't have a smart phone then. I knew the patron saint of eyes was Lucy, a martyr who had her eyes plucked out, but I didn't have any idea about the patron saint of legs. She said, 'You don't really believe in all that though, you don't think it will make a difference?' I paused and then said 'Probably not but, look anyway'. It's Saint Servatius if you ever need to know.

I've got a stone on my windowsill, with three perfect holes clean through it. When you hold it on its side it looks like a cartoon ghost. I call it Ghost Rock. I picked it up on the stoney beach at Lindisfarne when I was a teenager. It would have been Easter. Or maybe September. Either way the wind was blowing in a direction that carried the mournful cries of the seal colonies across from Outer Farne. I was telling myself a story about selkies. I was trying to remember something someone once told me about seals being the re-incarnated souls of sailors lost at sea. That's when I found Ghost Rock, it was half-comic and half-profound, exactly how I like things. So I kept it. Half as a talisman, half as a joke.

You see what's happening here. I'm explaining myself. This is the rational case. A woman, brought up on a diet of Catholicism and family holidays to the northeast coast is shut in a room for three weeks and conjures an image stitched together from things that have brought her comfort in the past.

I do not believe I had a vision in April 2020. I do not believe I accessed a profound truth.

I went in to a darkened room and I came out with what I took in, didn't I?

And yet.

And yet.

Part of me still yearns for that kind of faith. I've always wanted the kind of faith that Indiana Jones has in *The Last Crusade* at the leap from the lions head. That Joyce Butterfield had when she wrote a letter to be read aloud at her funeral and ended it with the words 'I'll see you all soon'.

Having MS made me believe in souls. It made me doubt my body, made me feel like this fleshy spacesuit is a Judas; unreliable, betrayer, nothing to do with who I am. I feel certain I have a soul, or a mind, an essential me-ness that's who I really am. I am to my body what a driver is to a car, a jockey to a horse. The way I feel certain that my body isn't me, I wish I could feel that certain about anything else. A religion. A lottery ticket. Anything at all.

We still live in a society that runs off faith, in ways we've learnt not to see. As a 17-year-old with no understanding of economics, the 2008 crash felt like a crisis of faith. From my perspective one day people believed in the market and everything was fine, the next day people lost their faith and everything tumbled down. The anti-vax crisis can be viewed as a crisis of faith in medical science. So many things in our world only work because we believe in them together: train timetables, the rules of a football game, traffic safety. I was in a car crash a few weeks ago, the roads are terrifying right now. I've lost my faith that other cars can pass mine with out calamity.

Consider time. Not real time, the tide, the pull of the moon, the earth spinning round the sun. Clock time, calendar time, made up time. In ancient Greece the nights had four hours and days had 12. In Britain the new year was in April until we changed our minds. In 1752 as the British Isles moved from the Julian to the Gregorian calendar we skipped 11 days, so people went to bed on the 2nd of September and woke up on the 14th.

Creativity runs on faith. Writing and making art is a kind of magic trick, just like flying in Neverland, Wile E. Coyote running past the edge of a cartoon cliff, the second you start to doubt you start to fall. I can suffer with horrible creative block, and it's all rooted in doubt. I spend weeks deleting every word I write, unpicking every stitch. It's not that I can't make anything, it's that I don't believe what I'm making is any good.

(from *Book of Hours*)

EVERYONE YOU KNOW
SOMEDAY WILL DIE

David Holzman

My Faustian Bargain: A Pianist Confronts Epilepsy

Midway through my first year of college, I began to experience what I called 'things'. That remained the banal title for years although *déjà vu* was also used on occasion by me and the friends to whom I described these episodes.

Déjà vu fitted well as it means *already seen* which was exactly what occurred though it did not describe my frightening reactions from beginning to end. *Seizure* is perfectly applicable because I would be 'seized', seemingly at random, by a visual image. I could be walking down the street and would be seized by a tree or a traffic sign. I could be seized by music notation, the windows in the front of my house (a common aura) or a face, seemingly for no reason, such as occurred at the train station, which I describe more fully later.

The image would well up and 'crawl' inside some part of my head (my gut would also feel it with a kind of emptiness). There was a magical, if sinister, intoxication, as though the image was bringing on some deeper reality, perhaps from far back in my past. There would be an almost sexual enticement—forcing me to stare ever-more-intensely at this image. At a certain point, the intensity would be so great that the image itself would begin to distort and perhaps break apart, often into a numeric or geometric shape. Music notation on the page would become bigger and spread beyond the page: a face would enlarge and I would focus upon a specific part of the face and the shape would seem magically like a Dali painting. A final acquiescence (or so it would seem) and I would lose consciousness.

Five to ten minutes later, I would regain my consciousness and then the frightening part would take place. I would not know what day it was, whether it was 9AM or 9PM, where I was or what I was there for. It is, for a few minutes, a state of utter helplessness and loss of terra firma.

Another five or six minutes later, reality would return, if not fully, close enough to feel consternation at myself for 'allowing' the seizure to occur. Then, I would go back to whatever task I was involved in—practicing piano, shopping, socializing, twice (only!) in fifty years performing.

After five years, I knew these events were called epilepsy. (I had been seeing a psychiatrist for five nears and the word epilepsy was never used.) At first, known as '*petit mal* seizures', they are now called 'focal/local partial epilepsy with impairment of consciousness' as my NYU Hospital web site describes it. In brief, it means that a part of my visual cortex was damaged (perhaps by the same virus that damaged my hearing) and that something, which no one has identified fully, will cause that particular minute portion of my brain to explode when a certain type of stress is placed upon it. These seizures were obviously more noticeable than partial deafness and could not be ignored.

The disturbance of these 'things' was mingled with excitement for several years as they seemed to mark me as especially sensitive. Perhaps this was because I loved *The Brothers Karamazov*, but it was, to a degree, an understandable response, and a sad defense, much like 'ownership' re deafness. I spent much time talking to others of the intricacies of this or that seizure and, as they were frequent for many years, I surely tarred myself with a brush which was to a degree unnecessary and, in hindsight, upsetting to the listener.

Additionally, as with hearing loss, it helped me create a sadly 'cool' and ironic personality, fit for the late '60's, because somewhere *not* so deep inside of myself, I was ashamed of this ailment, especially since I thought (as my parents surely did) that I could 'just say no' to the visual aura which preceded the seizure. I recall that if I were simply staring ahead dreamily, my father would come up to me and harshly comment 'hey, snap out of it'. Dreaminess had been part of my personality pre-epilepsy and even pre-hearing loss, but the soup was growing more complex as the various components mingled.

The musical side effects were, I believe, not that major (other than the means taken to prevent seizures!). Seizures destroyed brain cells and my memory, especially for names and faces, was poor. Most significant, and more noticeable now that seizures are relatively mild and much fewer, is the week-long after-effect. Melancholy, fatigue, upset stomach . . . simply an inability to function at my best.

There is indeed a body cycle which for at least two decades has been noticeable and almost predictable. About ten days of normality, ten days of being at my best in terms of quickness, physical state, mental alertness and musicality. Then, the slow imposition of a strange and dominant emotion, often felt as the constant hearing of a particular piece of music—lyrical, simple and from my younger years i.e. nostalgia and melancholy *sweet sorrow.* I can hear '*Tonight*' from *West Side Story, Deep River* with Paul Robeson's wonderful voice or *People Will Say We're in Love* from *Oklahoma.* I will tell Agnes with a smile that I am 'vulnerable' and a few days later, a seizure or perhaps two will occur.

Sometime in the middle of 2116, a new melody began to haunt me—*A New Created World* from Haydn's oratorio *The Creation.* It seemed to run parallel to the optimism I was feeling as the first positive results of the cochlear implant were discernable. The melody itself was very reminiscent of *Tonight,* and all of the music was strengthening.

In addition, the music struck deep personal chords. Robeson's ever-present voice in our house (and my father's connection to him at the famous Peeksvill riot in the early '50s); my intense fear at the witnessing of the ballet *Out of My Dreams and Into Your Arms* from *Oklahoma* which I saw with my mother in the late '50s; *West Side Story* which I saw when I was 13 with my sister and her friends (the gunshot at the end was an enduring shock); *The Creation,* which I worked on as pianist with the chorus at the High School of Music and Art. I strongly sense that these and various other memories were meant as strengthening agents as the brain recognized the imminence of seizure and looked for a wall of simplicity, optimism and love to protect me from the complex emotions which seizures brought on.

Neurologists are reluctant to posit guesses regarding the nature of epilepsy, admitting that they are still at a primitive stage of understanding (much as audiologists admit their limited knowledge of how the brain understands music). Stress is surely a factor, but I have found that the reduction of stress, whether over an hour or a day, can be as strong a factor in a seizure as vice-versa. I also will ask them, without getting an answer, which comes first—the brain explosion or the fastening upon an image? My hunch is that the explosion comes first and that therefore there is no need for a psychiatric explanation of what a particular image conveys to one's mind.

I can describe my seizures from the inside but will close with the description of one as seen from the outside, by one who has seen perhaps a hundred of my seizures, my dear and departed friend Agnes. The following is what she recently described to me about a seizure from 2004.

Agnes was driving me to Long Island University in Greenvale where I was to give a Convocation at Hillwood Commons (I am Professor there) at 1PM. I got a seizure perhaps ten minutes from the school while she was driving on Northern Boulevard. As she describes it, I got white, my head collapsed and I lost consciousness. She kept driving, now in the slow lane, and kept an eye on me in case of worsening.

Five to eight minutes later, I started to come out of it. I looked around and said "What's going on? I don't understand . . . where do I have to go?" It was like I was trying to connect past and present. Whatever Agnes said did not penetrate . . . so she said "relax". Ten to fifteen minutes later, I was still not back to reality . . . still asking . . .

She arrived at Hillwood, saw a colleague of mine, but knew to say nothing. She pulled into parking lot and I said "What's the matter with you?" She said "It's nice and sunny, let's enjoy it!"

Suddenly, I hit my head with my hand and said: "My God—I have to give a lecture . . . I left the car and walked to Hillwood. She saw me right before the lecture—I looked great . . . color back, talking and playing excellently in front of a full house of people.

10/27/17 Medicine is having a (perhaps too) strong effect and yoga is calming me down. I was sitting in a chair and felt the beginning of a seizure. It began in my gut, which my yoga instructor told me is a big bundle of nerves. I very clearly felt it rise slowly up to my eyes where I did indeed fasten upon a visual object. Then I felt it continue seemingly upward to my brain. It petered out before my brain could acquiesce but the path of the journey seemed clear. What is the GUT?

I am writing this at sixty-eight years of age. Medication has, for now, provided me a fairly satisfactory protection against seizures. But it was seldom so reliable or comfortable. In the recent past, seizures were stronger, more frequent, and a permanent cloud on my daily life (much as hearing loss still is . . .).

For me, seizures can occur anytime and anywhere, though usually with warnings. They most often occur when alone, and after some intense experience. I have somehow learned to deal with them safely (knock on wood). Often, they occur in the presence of a friend, which is fine for me. All of my friends are aware of my condition and know to do nothing but watch over me for the ten minutes or so before I regain consciousness. A short spell of relaxed talk and all is back to normal.

They will occasionally occur with people who are unaware of my condition, such as students, colleagues or people living on the block whom I would say hello to and make small talk. One piano student witnessed a seizure during a lesson at my college. He requested a new piano teacher. My neighbor witnessed one as I was walking up the hill and looking at a tree which caused the seizure. He called 911 I suppose and when the police came, I was unaware that I could refuse, thus finding myself in an emergency room with countless other people waiting for a doctor. At the front of the room was a bored-looking nurse. I waited for an hour, burst out laughing and left, vowing never to do that again.

I now know that I should tell individuals or groups what might occur, and it is not just protection, but the creation of a bond. It instantly eliminates fear, as they see a confident and relaxed person describing himself with a smile.

The most difficult and, at times, dangerous situations are seizures in wide-open spaces with people and/or vehicles all around. Places such as a street, a store, a concert hall or a train station. These are what my neurologist calls 'public seizures'. I have had several in the past decade and they have been emotionally and professionally damaging. Indeed, one was life-threatening. Three of these stand out as memories which will remain with me—one with black humor, one with bitterness and one with unfathomable wonder and life-changing consequences.

First, some background.

I was a very talented red-diaper baby. At four, I was playing folk songs as sung by Paul Robeson or The Weavers on my parents' Krakauer upright. At six, I was studying piano and marching the students into Assembly with improvised music. It was not long before Sonatinas and Prokofiev's *Music for Children* were part of my repertoire.

When I lost 90% of the hearing in my left ear at the age of nine, it didn't change the direction of my life. It was surely a personal and social disaster, but the musical fallout took a very long time to recognize and still longer to overcome. Oliver Sacks describes my symptoms precisely in his essay "In Living Stereo".

At eighteen, I started getting epileptic seizures, called *petit mal* as they were not the stronger seizures. These were explosions in my visual cortex and the expression *déjà vu* stayed with me for a long time. These were intoxicating, magical and ultimately frightening fixations upon a visual image—a tree, a musical score, a face . . . once the image had me in its grip, for several years with my enthusiastic acquiescence, later despite my efforts to escape, I would be forced to stare ever more intensely at an object which seemed more than just itself—rather a superhuman friend or foe. I would feel that I was repeating my life somehow, hence *déjà vu* . The more intense the interaction, the more the image would become distorted and surrealistic. At some point, it (and I) would explode, leaving me unconscious for ten minutes and confused for five more.

For many years, I would do what many people with seizures do—talk about it too much. Thus, as with hearing loss, seizures narrowed my life. I slowly recognized the body and chemical cycle which gave a shape to epilepsy. It was a five-week cycle (now perhaps a shorter and weaker cycle) in which there were high points, low points (the immediate days afterwards) and, most strangely, warning signs. For several years, if I heard too much *West Side Story* (especially *Tonight*) in my head I would become very nostalgic, near tears, and I would know that seizures were imminent. Later, *Oklahoma* and *A New Created World* from Haydn's *Creation* served the same function. A lovely and simple melody would be my brain's way of protecting against the oncoming chaos.

Pianistically, the damage came from the medications used then (and now) to limit seizures. I suspected from the beginning that there was a sluggishness which arose from these pills, whichever the name at the time. When my piano teacher Paul Jacobs saw me take a pill (I was almost bragging to him that I needed medicine) he asked me what it was. I told him it was librium. He looked concerned and said "That slows you down". I replied "You can see that it doesn't". He replied "I'm not so sure". Thus, a few years after seizures began, the focus was more on the cure than the illness.

Again, I was not deterred musically. I knew what music meant and what music meant most—20th Century music. I was clearly able to overcome the complexities of this music and play it with clarity and spontaneity. Indeed, my pianistic personality was surely built upon my handicaps. Still, playing with the top freelancers in town, I felt that I was a tiny notch behind them. Learning was a bit slower, reacting was less natural and hearing their parts clearly was a greater effort for me than it seemed for them. Partly, it was being a pianist rather than an experienced ensemble player, but part was surely my handicaps. Those who knew me best were aware of my issues and spared a little extra rehearsal time to overcome this. Those whom I worked with but did not know as friends probably did not know—but I often wonder if a person can hide anything from others.

When I was about forty, my musical needs and my vanity prompted me to complain more vehemently than ever before to my neurologist about the mental, digital and visual roadblocks caused by my medicine. I was performing some of the most difficult music to be found and I blamed medicine, in part, for my struggles. I went on a shopping spree of trying different medicines, always seeking a miracle—no or few seizures and a return to the full responsiveness I thought I saw in others and in my own past. It was a fool's errand.

One medicine produced double vision after several hours. This was present in several rehearsals and concerts. Another made me want to jump out of my front window. A third had no side effects. However, it did not control seizures, as I found out when I had a seizure on my bicycle and lost much of the hearing in my right ear.

My career in ensemble music came to a pretty much immediate end as I could barely hear. While a hearing aid was of some use for speech, it was of no use for music. My teaching and solo career continued seemingly as before, but something had clearly gone out of my life. I changed neurologist, found the one medicine that I think of with affection—Keppra—but added the one I think of with hate—lamictal. And for several years, life was as sluggish as the medication intended it to be. Few seizures, emotional blandness and loss of motivation.

Until 1998: Austin Clarkson of the Stefan Wolpe Society called to ask if I would make an Wolpe cd for Bridge Records, as part of their celebration of his Centennial. I was thrilled with the prospect and soon realized that I would have to take my handicaps fully into account to both learn this complex music (I had only learned his feared *Battle Piece*, the rest of the music was utterly new to me) and to perform it at the level of electricity and communication it required. I needed a fully active brain and nervous system to 'hear' notes I could not hear. I needed the fullest intensity to overcome the harmonic and rhythmic complexities and I needed full command of my fingers, indeed all of my body from eyes to toes, to fully master these works.

I could not, I knew, achieve that with a full dosage of lamictal; hence, with my new neurologist's acquiescence, I went from 250 mgs to 150 mgs. I would accept the risks for the sake of giving my life back its meaning.

This Faustian bargain was at first most noticeable when practicing these many challenging works in front of me. First, Wolpe, but soon Roger Sessions, Ralph Shapey and many others. This connection was utterly understandable and perhaps even predictable.

One result of my Faustian bargain with lower lamictal dosages was an increase in seizures. This was most noticeable while practicing the many works which I would be learning, performing and recording. It was utterly understandable and even predictable. The increase in my intensity, the hours spent, combined with the further hearing loss surely created a stressful experience for my eyes, ears, fingers and my emotions. The challenges and the rewards were seldom as clear as during this fifteen-year stretch. What was unpredictable was that these seizures became an accepted part of what was a well-ordered life by my standards, centered upon the six hours of pianistic efforts.

In 2008, I described this experience in the postlude to my essay "Musical Freefall" which concerned my experiences projecting the time-space in Wolpe's *Battle Piece*. Austin Clarkson suggesting saving this postlude for my memoirs and I include an excerpt below.

Where I am still occasionally vulnerable to seizures is when sitting at the piano practicing complex new music. Most specifically, I must be careful in the afternoon, after a few hours of practice and when working on stages two, three and four of practice regimen. The reason seems to be the 'friction' involved in these steps, where I must slowly and intensely think backwards as well as up-and-down for poly-rhythms (finding the proper fingering requires thinking backwards as does phrase gestures and dynamics).

When I am at the low point in a five-week cycle (I now recognize warning signals days in advance), I can find myself practicing and alarms will flash in both my abdomen and in some part of my brain describing an unsettling feeling of emptiness. This is often connected with a micro-sluggishness, which means a reluctance to move my hands to a new position. I usually say to myself 'finish the page and then take a break'. This is good enough, if I am lucky, but occasionally, five minutes later, I could write a fingering into the score, or see a complex web of lines, and the score will turn into a magical image as a true seizure begins. I still have time to react and, with strong will-power, I force my head away from the score to look out the window. I put a smile on my face and look upwards at what I tell myself is a beautiful and peaceful sight, and calmly walk away from the piano and sit down, with what appears to be little effect beyond fatigue though my close friend Agnes will see or hear me later and somehow know.

If, however, I am very tired, melancholy or worried about my musical career (given my repertoire, it happens often enough), I will give in and 'allow' the seizure to take place ('allow' has the same degree of vagueness as 'hemiola' because a complete seizure probably includes my 'allowance'). While the seizure offers a temporary respite from the tension, it takes no then a few minutes to regret my 'weakness' and strengthen my resolve to stop next time at the most minute warning—a technique of repetition which I learned from practicing and which is slowly but surely winning out.

I quoted Emerson above ("When walking on thin ice, one's best defense is speed") because this never occurs in performances or in any up-to-tempo playing. 'Friction' and self-consciousness are the factors that allow a minor chemical imbalance to grow to a seizure. While I would be happier if these occurrences were entirely vanquished, they are rare enough and mild enough to live with. Most important, the result of all the musical effort is a true 'multi-dimensional reality', unlike the chaotic unreality of seizures.

I should note that my assertion that seizures never occur during performances was disproved a few years later and, additionally, I now have a better recognition of what brings them on.

What perhaps needs more description is the physical and emotional landscape in which I worked during those years. Not only was my chamber music career dissolved due to further hearing loss, but my family was also disappearing. In the early 1990s I was living with two aging but still active parents, experiencing their shrinking world the way most people do.

By the mid-90s, I would be practicing and in the corner of my field of vision, I would see my father playing pinochle by himself on the couch in the living room. He was a proud and defensive person who found it hard to admit frailty. He was, in fact, a lonely old man who was secretly getting strength from seeing and hearing his son making music, though he could not say so to me directly (perhaps not yet to himself either). I knew it and yet blocked it from my thoughts and kept practicing, immersed in my challenges.

Five years later, he would still be on the couch, now most often asleep (my mother maintained an active life longer than he did). I still saw him out of the corner of my eye and it seemed easier to block out my thoughts and feelings, as if he were an inert object. Five years later, the couch was empty. My parents were living the remaining few years of their lives in an old-age home and I was alone in a quiet house and a quiet neighborhood with brothers in distant cities.

In addition to the body cycle which brought on seizures, they seemed at this point in my life, to serve an almost family function. When vulnerable in late afternoons, my 'wait!' was almost a game, as though I were joking with my younger brother in the far distant past, whether watching *Plan X From Outer Space* or playing *Stratego*. The seizures also seemed a validation of my efforts and my goals, as if a heavenly piano teacher was approving of my effort on this day. The 'game' of these seemingly innocent seizures was, of course, an illusion, as I found out soon after.

AFTERTHOUGHT: Of all the composers I worked on over this stretch, it seems in hindsight that the music of Roger Sessions was the most powerful path to seizures. The intricacies of fingering and the complexities of the counterpoint were surely part, but I always seemed to feel a special emotional pang when experiencing his music.

The music reflected his personality to the small extent that I had known him and even seeing his face in a photograph. Whatever the brilliance, violence or lyricism in the music, I felt a reserve. Whether this was patrician dignity or, more likely, a pervasive melancholy, I did not know. But I felt it my duty to overcome this reserve and create spontaneous and ebullient experiences for myself and the listener. Wolpe was always direct, Shapey always had a grotesque lightheartedness. Other composers I simply experienced less fully.

Sessions, like my father lying on the couch, was holding something back. Perhaps that extra need to reach inside him emotionally made the intensity of the effort yet more dangerous.

The 'public seizures' which I alluded to earlier, did not suddenly begin during this period. I recall one during a performance when I was a Masters student. I recall another at about the same time during a group therapy session (I was taken out of the group as I apparently frightened other members). There were surely others but none seemed significant of memorable until the following three.

Seizures can occur anytime and anywhere, though usually with warnings. For me, they most often occur when alone and after some intense experience. I somehow have learned to deal with them safely (knock on wood). Often, they occur with a friend, which is fine for me. All of my friends are aware of my condition and know to do nothing but watch over me for the ten or so minutes before I regain consciousness. A short spell of relaxed talk and all is back to normal.

They will occasionally occur with people unaware of my condition such as students, colleagues or neighbors. I have frightened many individuals who see a seizure. One student at LIU requested a new piano teacher; a neighbor from half a block away (whom I would say hello to and smile), saw a seizure while I was walking up the hill and looking at the tree. He called for an ambulance and I was unaware that I could refuse, thus finding myself in an emergency room will countless other people awaiting a doctor. At the front of the room was a bored-looking nurse. I waited for an hour, burst out laughing and left, vowing never to do that again. I now know that I should tell individuals or groups what might occur, and it is not just protection but the creation of a bond. It instantly eliminates fear, as they see a confident and relaxed person describing himself with a smile.

The most difficult and, at times, dangerous, situations are seizures in wide-open spaces with people and/or vehicles all around- such as a street, a store, a concert hall or a train station. These are what my former neurologist called 'public seizures' in 2012. I had several such seizures in the past decade and they had been emotionally and professionally damaging. Indeed, one was life-threatening.

Lower medication was surely a factor. Stress which was piling up on all sides must have been another. Whatever the complex soup, my doctor ultimately saw a situation which could not be allowed too continue. This would lead to a massive change in my life.

Three of these 'public seizures' stand out as memories which will remain—one with a sparkle of sad humor, one with pain, and one with unfathomable wonder.

I entered Chatham Square Music School in 1961 and started studying piano with Augusta Scheiber, a warm and musical woman who lived in a brownstone on Bank Street. It was my introduction to the West Village and, while I never walked west of 8th Avenue, I discovered Bleecker Street and Corner Bistro. I brought my Schirmer's Edition of the Beethoven Sonatas with me and she wrote on the inside cover: *Patelson's Music Shop 160 W56th Street.* Thus began my half-century relationship with the store that many musicians knew as a second-home. They could walk in and simply look in the stacks of music—piano in the front, books in the middle and I don't precisely know how the back was organized. There was also a staircase which led to used scores, making it the 'half-price music store'. There were young musicians working there. There was Joseph Patelson, a kindly elderly man with the time to converse with seemingly everyone. And there was Mrs. Patelson (I did not know for quite a while that they were married). She was more grim, with piercing eyes, no smile, and clearly ran the place. I was always a bit afraid of her and probably never said a word to her for forty years.

In 2005, I needed to find various works by Jewish emigres from the Holocaust for concerts in Washington and Goethe Institut in New York. One of the works was by Eric Zeisl—*November Pieces* which was out of print. I naturally went to Patelsons to look for it. I found myself face-to-face with Mrs. Patelson and we walked up to the second floor to look for old copies. I had never been on the second floor, and walking up the old wooden staircase with this unworldly being made me feel that I was participating in a fairy tale, as though ascending through the clouds to a new world, being led by a cunning half-human. Sure enough, on opening a draw in a dusty cabinet, there was the Zeisl, an old musty score.

BUT THAT IS WHERE THE STORY STOPS. I was staring into the drawer and a seizure came over me. I assume it lasted the usual amount of time and the next thing I recall was walking down the steps and seeing two policemen waiting for me. My wits were slowly returning and I knew that I would not let them take me to an ER. I also began to remember that I had an appointment to meet a friend on Broadway and 72nd Street for lunch.

After a tense twenty minutes, I signed the white sheet absolving the city from responsibility and left. I have no recollection of whether I left with the music I had come for—I don't see how I could have paid for it, but I have an old musty score of the music so who knows?

My strangest memory was of leaving the store. I was not yet fully myself. My balance was bad and I kept one hand on the glass wall of the building on 57th Street between 7th Ave and Broadway (Chase Bank?). By Columbus Circle, my sense of direction had returned and I indeed ended up on Broadway and 72nd. That was that! Ps: My friend noticed nothing.

A day or two later, I called my doctor to tell him what happened. When I said that I refused to go to a hospital, he exclaimed happily "Good for you!" That was news to me as I expected him to chide me, but it was strengthening. I was indeed master of my fate.

Many months later, I either needed music, or needed an excuse to revisit Patelson's. It was very difficult to gather the courage to go there and face what I thought would be hostility or pity. I felt much the way I did when walking up the hill on my block and, for years lacking the ability to look at the tree that caused the seizure that my neighbor saw and acted upon by calling the police. I summoned the courage, opening the door, walked down the two or three steps and found myself back in the store. Sure enough, there was Mrs. Patelson, with what looked to me like an even more stony gaze, as if saying 'how dare you disturb my peace?' I left soon after and never returned. A year or two later, the store was gone. Mr. Patelson had died and this home for musicians was no longer.

Strangely, with new medicine, I had the courage to stare at the menacing tree. All went well. The image of a large somewhat barren tree facing me from afar no longer inspired any reaction in my brain. Soon after, the tree itself was gone, whether due to a gas leak, or simply being chopped down, I do not know. Now, I will occasionally stare at the empty spot and try to summon an image in my brain to see if I can re-create any of the magic. I cannot. The medicine is utterly triumphant and the visual aura that haunted me for so many years is gone. I do not feel any nostalgia for those 'good old days' but I do miss Patelson's.

Bargemusic had become a vital part of New York's musical life before the turn of the Century. Olga Bloom had turned a coffee barge into a 'floating concert hall' in Fulton Ferry Landing and Mark Peskanov was the Artistic Director. Soon after discovering its existence, I realized the great interest they had in modern repertoire. I contacted Mark and gave my first recital there in 2008 as part of their 'New American Music' series. I would be promoting myself, my recordings and the composers who were closest to me personally and musically.

For my premiere performance, I did what a responsible performer would do—I played musical 'friends'. That meant music which I had performed often and knew well. It included music of Ralph Shapey and Roger Sessions, which I had recorded for Bridge Records. It included music of Wolpe, always a friend, a short work of Pozzi Escot, a dear friend, and the Carter Sonata, a work which for some reason required no more than a day's preparation despite its length and complexity. I must have learned it when my mind and spirit were at their height.

Meeting Olga Bloom at the concert was similar to meeting Irma Wolpe decades earlier. Olga Bloom was a dignified lady, more Russian than American. I greeted her and she told me that 'the New York Times is here'. I replied with what I thought was self-deprecatory wit and said 'well, that makes me nervous' with a smile. She stiffly said something like 'you are not supposed to get nervous! You must play your best!' My recollection is that I assured her that I would and then simply readied myself to perform.

It was a success (the Carter did its job as it was singled out for praise) and I was invited to return the following season. I did so and now began including newer works by composers such as John Harbison and Shulamit Ran mixed in with my friends Wolpe and Sessions (different works than the previous year). The Harbison Sonata was only my second performance and was still a struggle in places. I felt, mistakenly, that anything less than full mastery, i.e. staring at the score, digital struggles, lack of spontaneity, made a performance to some degree a failure. I felt that here, but he was largely happy and the notion that effort is indeed part of a performance began to take root in my consciousness, though I am not yet fully persuaded that anything less than 'effortless' is not somehow to be apologized for.

The third concert, in 2010, contained two major challenges to go with several friends, including Bartok's *Out of Doors* and excerpts from Messaien's *Vingt Regard sur l'Enfant-Jesus,* works which I had performed for decades. The challenges were Eric Moe's *Three Ways to Relieve Tension* and Elmar Lampson's *Per Axion Esti,* an American premiere.

Both were plain and simply VERY DIFFICULT . . . Moe was a scintillating Mendelssohnian scherzo in modern dress. Lampson was a contrapuntally complex work combining Wolpe's rhythmic independence and Messaien's three-staff chordal writing. In addition, the notation of both works was smaller than usual and after cataract surgery a few months prior, my vision was as much a handicap as my hearing. Thus, I was not really the master of either—they were not memorized, my fingers could not easily find the chords in Lampson and my eyes could not look ahead easily in the fast-moving Moe. After a short work of Ursula Mamlok opened the program, these two closed the first half. I remember telling my page-turner 'if I get through the first-half I am home-free'. This was reminiscent of an all-Martino concert fifteen years ago at Miller Theater. I was struggling with the double-vision described above, and I told my page-turner that if I was lucky the double-vision would not occur until the final work, which I had largely memorized. I was exactly right and the concert was a great success.

Unlike the Martino concert, my prediction here proved wrong. I got through the first half better than I expected, though with intense effort. The second half began with Bartok and indeed, all was a piece of cake. Until the last movement, *Chase.* Halfway through the piece, with its cascading left hand sixteenth notes, and its right hand violent melody, I felt a seizure coming on. It was probably the score that created the aura—I don't remember. I did what I often did when practicing—I kept going, desperately trying to ignore the oncoming explosion while keeping up the left-hand quintuplets. At a certain point, the seizure won. I stopped, was probably unconscious for the usual amount of time, and, unfortunately, a degree of destructive chaos took over the hall.

My friends, and my neurologist, who often attended my concerts, knew what had happened, and tried to tell the audience to stay put and be patient. The people in the control room did not understand and turned off the lights and stopped recording the event. Thus, half the audience left and half stayed.

I did recover and apparently my friends persuaded the people in the control room to let the concert proceed. Thus, lights were turned back on and, with half the audience, I finish the concert. My only memory, confirmed by my former teacher Louis Martin who was present, is that the first piece I played, utterly unintentionally, was the Schubert *G flat Impromptu*—not on the program, but one of my most beloved friends which I first learned a half a century ago (Louis told me it was a beautiful performance). I then played Messaien, though I have no recollection of it, and only remember being driven home by my friend Jonathan, who turned pages.

I should note that this utterly unexpected seizure seems to confirm my sense that seizures often occur when there is a steep and rapid decline in stress. All my mental efforts went into the first half. It must have been a precipitous fall into the comfort zone that followed that allowed this to occur.

I never performed at Bargemusic again. I tried to contact Mark once or twice, with the same difficulty as opening the door of Patelson's. It is necessary to realize that these sad consequences are understandable, and to allow common sense to be triumphant over one's emotions. I do recognize more than I ever did that he, like others whom I have had experiences with, to the extent that he remembers me, wishes me well and respects me and then goes about his own life. I will take a train to attend a concert at Barge and will, I am pretty sure, enjoy myself among people and music. The memory is still there, but it is not noxious, and I cannot let such memories poison my life.

In April of 2012, I woke up and casually enjoyed a morning of breakfast, newspaper, telephone, shower, shave and a touch of piano playing. I would be giving a lecture/recital with my colleague Austin Clarkson at Columbia University at 3PM on the music of Stefan Wolpe. It was a casual and pleasant mood because I had the rare blessing of playing and discussing music I had performed often and recently recorded—a breeze compared to first performances.

I would follow my new routine: avoid buses and #7 subway, walk to the Bayside Station of Long Island Railroad and catch a noon train. That way, I would arrive early, have lunch, find the Music Building, and perhaps socialize a bit—all without looking nervously at my watch. I got to the station early, and events quickly began to conspire against my relaxation and indeed became surrealistic. My best recollection provides the following.

I was waiting on the Eastbound platform, presumably due to track work on the regular side. I looked up at a large ad on the wall of a building nearby. Now, what should not have happened, happened. The woman's face on the ad grabbed me and would not let me go. This aura grew more intense. I tried to look away and keep relaxed and thinking of other things, but after a vain effort, I imploded. An epileptic seizure at the worst possible moment.

The next thing I knew, I was walking on the railroad tracks—Westbound, towards the city— blithely, as if in a dream. What will always leave me clueless is: HOW IN THE WORLD SOMEONE WITH POOR BALANCE MANEUVERED FIVE FEET DOWN TO THE

TRACKS WITH MY ATTACHE CASE STILL ON MY SHOULDER.

I kept walking. A few minutes later, the world seemed to be returning a little. I saw a man on the street above the tracks waving to me to get off the tracks and climb up the hill. At first, I thought he was saying hello. A few minutes later, I realized he had a point—it was dangerous. I looked for a location to get off tracks, found one, casually walked up the hill, found a hole in the fence and found myself on Station Road.

My memory was beginning to return and I realized that I was there to catch a train to New York—I did not yet remember why. So, with a bit of difficult logic, ie. 2+2=4, I turned around and walked back to the station, ready to catch the next Westbound train. By now, I was fully conscious of where I was going, what I was going for and when I had to be there. Thus, urgency and concern began to creep into my being.

At the station, however, there were two policemen waiting for me. I had by now returned to reality and I knew what the script would be and what I would have to do to reach Columbia University.

The police wanted to take me to a local hospital. This had happened to me several times. The first time, I was timid and naïve (I thought I had to go) as described above, but knew to never let it happen again.

This time, with urgency and rising vehemency, I told them that this has happened before and, as they can see, I am recovered. I showed them the piano scores which I was to perform and I am not sure what effect that had for good or bad (fittingly, one work was called *Stehendemusik* or 'timeless music'—an apt description of a seizure). However, after thirty minutes of fruitless talk (my doctor was unreachable), the magic pieces of white paper were served for me to sign. While I never read them fully and barely heard the offices' talk, the gist was that I signed an agreement stating that I was allowed to go, and any dangers or incidents were my responsibility—not the city of New York.

Thus, I waited a while for the next train, anxiously staring at my watch and frantically calculating the probable length of the trip. All memories of the LIRR, the 7th Avenue Express, the 7th Avenue local and the hectic search for the Music Building are gone . . . the next thing I remember is entering the lecture room about eight minutes late, and seeing Austin's eyes wide in astonishment. I never knew whether it was my clothing or my face that showed the odyssey, but as always, something remained denoting seizure. After a few self-conscious minutes of lecture, I performed Wolpe's dizzying *Waltz for Merle* with aplomb and thereafter was sharp, witty, i.e. myself.

After a brief dinner with Austin (I never told him what happened and I do not know if he guessed) and perhaps others, I took the local and express downtown and the LIRR Eastbound to Bayside and walked home. It was a fitting 'spiegelbild' or 'mirror-image' common in Wolpe's music and an apt metaphor for the day's events.

Once on the railroad, I could relax and let my thoughts stay with me. I knew that what had happened marked the end of another stage in my battle with epilepsy. For several years, I had engaged in a Faustian bargain with the acquiescence of my neurologist. I would take less of a particularly handicapping medication (lamictal) in order to learn, perform and record many challenging modern keyboard masterpieces. The risks of more and perhaps more intense seizures would be accepted for the sake of reaching the speed, energy, precision i.e. the MASTERY which the music required.

I reached home and, for two days, told no one. I let the indisputable facts and logic reach me before talking. This was the third such 'public seizure' which had occurred in the past few years, but never before had my life been on the line. I contacted my neurologist who seemed both shocked and admiring. Second, my fellow Queens resident and close friend George. I told him while he was driving—a mistake as he almost drove off Lefferts Boulevard. I waited several days before telling my dearest companion Agnes and indeed left it at that—a bridge to be crossed.

The 'bridge to be crossed', not for the first nor for the last time, was, indisputably, safeguarding myself from such events. It meant increasing the dosage of lamictal, and, a few months later (after completing a CD) adding yet another medication. I was not in a position to argue or play coy with those basic facts.

Hence began a new chapter, and the most distressing to experience and even write about. I would go through the same debate a year later. Much like the Mozart *A minor Rondo*, the variations of the ever-returning theme could not hide the melancholy, and the contrasting sections, even though in 'happy' major keys, were all tinted by the same motif. For me, hearing loss and epilepsy tint daily life, but music and the successful efforts to bring it to life, will give me strength and wisdom and I slowly realize have already allowed for a resolution in the tonic.

Doug Smith

Waiting

Nick was one of eight mentally disabled men living in the house. For him, the thing he anticipated the most was his weekly walk with his dad. Every Friday at two o'clock his dad came to the house and the two of them went on a long walk around the neighborhood. Every Friday at one o'clock, Nick came down from his second-floor bedroom to stand behind the front door, coat draped over his arm, waiting for his dad. He would wait the hour until his dad came, then the two of them would go out on that walk, each of them talking and playfully kidding one another and laughing.

Nick's dad became ill and had to miss an occasional Friday. Yet, every Friday at one o'clock, Nick went down from his bedroom and stood behind the front door, coat draped over his arm, waiting for his dad. When his dad did not come, Nick would take his coat back up to his room and anxiously wait for the next Friday.

Nick's dad died. For over seven years, until Nick himself died, every Friday at one o'clock Nick went down from his bedroom and stood behind that front door, coat draped over his arm, waiting for his dad.

Lauren Foley

Penitential Acts

Breathless. Spoken. / = beat
// = pause
— = run-on lines

: // = abrupt pause

I confess to almighty God / and to you / my brothers and sisters / that I have sinned through my own fault / in my thoughts and in my words / in what I have done / and in what I have failed to do / and I ask blessèd Mary / ever Virgin / all the angels and saints / and you / my brothers and sisters / to pray for me to the Lord our God / in the upper echelons of this faith they drink the fruits / our earthly labour / which human hands hath made / begotten not made / of one being with the Father // Lie here // striking shadows cast by clouds turning and twisting above / me / Stretch out / on backs considering skyscape / plucked from the vine / grapes / which human hands have made / see through its taut transparent skin / see its veins / peel back the burgundy cover / succulent and wet to its core / in my / where the seed is hard / in my thoughts / covered by this fleshy extremity / in my thoughts / the oval spot concealed by this flesh / blessèd flesh / in my thoughts / blessèd are you among women / in what I have done / in thought / and blessèd is the fruit of your womb // sunkissed // And in what I have failed to do—weather-beaten fruitless harvest a decrepitude of old men's impotence—what have I what have I done—lonely only beauty of youth—I ask—full of plucking ripe for the picking—pluck my impotence of now—what have I done—I have done—subdue the music be with the heart the bosom—lie down—here—under our earthly labour—I have done undone—I have warmed to the flicker with heat and move next to me in the vine we are one to be done and undone—what have I—I have // burned with the dance and you're close so close so close the ripeness lie here on your back rest lay your head on me you are ripe for the plucking from this vine and music be the heart of dance and: // what have I have have done I have done and: // the fruit of this vine is next to be plucked by hands we have made and ready to pluck the flesh your flesh my flesh and lubricate ourselves and the fruit of the union spontaneous growth—fruition—we consecrate this vine with a stupor a passion a flame a hell and Burn Burn Burn for all your mortal sins ashes to ashes dust to dust—a new test— // And I ask blessèd Mary all the angels and saints to pray for us sinners now and at the hour of our death: // through our fault through our fault through our most grievous fault

(From *Polluted Sex*, Influx press, 2022)

Lynn Buckle

H is for Plane

You fingerspell H.E.R.O.N. in Irish Sign Language, holding nature-writing clichés in your right hand. It could have been otter, tree, or startled doe. Or the blood, bone, and sedge of curlewed eco poetry. Dolphins rarely feature now, as your gaze falls upon the familiar trends of wild hawks and wilier foxes, snails even, lizards on dry stone walls too old and over-climbed by writers' words. You write fondly of these tropes; the soft-drug creatures of conservation; entry level stuff. And of problematic deer needing problematic wolves to contain them. You give explanations about stunted tree growth and are accused of exposition, and sign

education as if putting your brain into another's.

Soon your nature writing becomes an @Deer_Eye petition to save the mountainy highlands slash deserts, then something about peatbog extraction (but only BSL has a dedicated sign for that so perhaps it isn't your problem?), and you want to create a sea grass theme park and run conserventure playgrounds. But that is far too complicated to sign so you organise fleets of plastic kayaks for ocean clean-ups instead. Dream of opening a bookshop on the slopes of Snowdonia for slow-queueing tourists, specialising in nature writing by doctors who rewilded their landed estates and academic doctors whose great-great grandfathers had working class trousers instead of Craghoppers. Squeeze more bucks please. Or not. Because you are deaf or

because you are white

you add the curative effects of forest bathing, wild swimming, or long-distance walking. Not to be confused with just going for a walk or a quick dip. In sign they really do look shit, like someone drowning or recalling something from Mabinogion's (fingerspell, book) timber armies marching towards transformative moments, mushrooms connecting. Petrichor (although the sign for that isn't great either). Waiting. To salve furrowed brows or you write escapist survivalist tripe. There are colonial seeds to unpack so you post videos of your organic garden on Instagram, delete clips of exotic flora & fauna from last year's Indonesia trip, exotic to whom? Then a follower reminds you about the Icelandic ones and, as you lie awake at night worrying about being cancelled and losing privilege, you regret flying to see bleached coral reefs. You wonder if you are really connecting with nature, and if there is too much Armageddon. You were told to be solution-based.

You draw a W down into a Y

because

you do not know the sign name for heron. Your vocabulary is limited, not just by your language. You dip into another, stepping carefully to poise, and settle on home-sign. An almost not-quite-there sign of

bird, grey, white, H in slow flight.

Hearing people not getting the irony

because

they do not know sign or because

soon you must write that the signs were there all along; that H.E.R.O.N. (finger-spelled softly) is nearly extinct, that it will be marked upon information boards made of re-cycled plastic, signposts set into concrete. Climate deniers not getting the irony

because

the sign for dead is very exact, if only they knew it. It cannot be missed or misconstrued or confused with alive when dead is all they've got and they were warned not to consume so much or to fly Ryannair. But they insisted on cheap holidays abroad, on cultural trips to Vienna and stags in New York. Oh deer. You spent your writing residency in Paris and pretended flying there didn't matter when you flagged it on social media, forgetting it was killing the

H.E.R.O.N.s of year 2044.

You will remember the sign for dead. You will remember the full-stops.

You still do not remember the ISL sign for heron.

Bird

is too small, insufficiently languorous, lacks the statuesque patience of a cliché erased.

You keep the H preternaturally horizontal for too long. There is no F into the future

because

we are at right-angles to it now.

Low sun, H flaps along (iconicity home-sign?), behind trees, silver on water.

Except that the sign for silver literally pushes itself upwards, exploding through imagined surfaces, dripping mercury and evening light, S's everywhere, ending in a single applause. So, you do not need to sign beautiful. And you do not need to make it so, in this place where trees cave-over river, where sanctuaries are made. Here, insects are many just because their sign name always says so and you wonder how many times you should nip the air when you are signing insects if their numbers are already diminished. You will do one less nip tomorrow. One less the day after that. And so on, until Friday, when it will be a non-existent sign and the word for insect will have disappeared from Irish Sign Language

because

we made it happen.

You fill the air instead, clouds of your insect sign, nipping like green peas. Your postman sees you signing, pulls over empty-handed, and enquires (in his quiet voice) about your flailing.

You talk about not failing the planet.

He points to the overhanging trees, the lush abundance, your wayward no-mow garden. Your bounty. He does not get your point; that every point and nip in your sign for insect is important for nature (in your loudest sign).

In the sign for nature

you see

fingers starting from a place where colours are signed; green, blue, red, pink, orange, brown, but not black

because the priests took that

water

which is close to coming from the place of plenty. Your optimistic language.

You even use nice with both hands. Not much is afforded that importance.

And two u's, meaning not just us but all the us's everywhere and that is about as inclusive as you could ever get, unlike everything

your fingers land where feelings start and wild cruelty expands, held so close that nature is you, not something othered. It is written into the grammar.

So, when others speak of language failing nature, you know they have not seen you sign. They do not know your twenty-five home-signs for river in different weathers as you adapt your flow, surface tension, colour, and hand movements. They have not seen the barometer of your heart spell H.E.R.O.N.

They send you photos instead, of herons standing one-legged or in low flight. You wish the senders would stop booking flights. You

wish H.E.R.O.N. heron (home-sign) life

and nature without an H full of planes.

Shahd Alshammari

My Better Half

I pulled her out of the medicine cabinet, after years of trying to keeping up with the world. At first, she scared me. Her presence made me reject her for the longest time, constantly shutting her back into the medicine cabinet. During the pandemic, I began to wonder whether she had more to offer than just sitting among my multiple supplements and medications. What if she could help me navigate the world? What if she was my compass?

Programming her to look and sound like me was not altogether difficult, albeit time-consuming. With my pressing chronic fatigue, I could only work on specific body parts at a time. By the time lockdown restrictions began to ease, she was complete. Ready to interact with the world.

I charged her constantly, through touch. I would place my hand on her skull, circling and tapping her forehead to awaken her. Charging her, I learned, was necessary to keep her from slowing down and nodding off in the middle of conversation. We slept in the same bed so that she could have access to my dreams. I programmed her to pretend to sleep the way that I did and recall my dreams in the morning (in case someone asked her what she had dreamt). She learned all of my moves, the twitches, the groaning, and yet did not feel the pain the way that I did. She was programmed without any pain censors. She could feel the whole array of emotions, and could even feel anger—but never physical pain. That way, she wouldn't disturb or make anyone feel uncomfortable in the presence of pain. She would only falter if she wasn't touched every 72 hours, and begin to yawn excessively. I made sure she was charged every day.

She began to come alive in the most beautiful way possible. Life size. Her skin was flawless, her eyes piercing and smart. I neglected to add the dark circles under her eyes to resemble my constant fatigue. She never fought back, never protested. A perfect creature.

She started teaching my classes on days I could not move a limb. Of course, no one noticed. When she returned from a long day of work, I would remove her tongue from her body and insert it into my phone to watch the entire narrative of the day. I didn't want to miss out on my life. It was as my students say—FOMO—except I didn't just fear it, I was stuck with an even worse dilemma. I was missing out on my own life by constantly having to cancel classes, miss out on family events, friends' birthdays, dinner dates, concerts, etc. You name it. I was always fatigued, stuck in bed.

I would wake up around 8:30 AM and have my morning black coffee with her. We smiled at each other, a strange connection of looking at myself without a mirror. Sometimes her hair would be done and mine would be messy. She had the energy to manage her curls (*our* curls, I should emphasize) and to dress sharply. I couldn't get out of my checkered pajamas. I had no choice but to send her instead. I lived through her and yet I still felt the fear of missing out on human interaction in my own life's narrative. I spent too much time on my phone, watching and replaying everything.

There were no glitches. Nobody noticed a thing.

In fact, as fate would have it (or it may have been my karma for messing with nature's laws), she was loved. Much loved. She was a marvelous and dedicated teacher, friend, daughter, sister, and a wonderful date. She never took any rest days, never let down a friend in need, took care of her aging parents, and was always great company.

I confess that I felt the pangs of jealousy surge. She was my better half. Better at my life.

Two years later, I stopped charging her and started thinking about phasing her out of my life's narrative. People would have to make do with the real me. I wasn't living an authentic life if I only lived through her. She had to go.

And here I am today, sprawled in bed, with her back in the medicine cabinet. I am unemployed, friendless, and loveless. I phased her out but, in the process, everyone around me left. They couldn't accommodate me when I had been perfectly accommodating for two whole years.

Sometimes I look into the medicine cabinet and think about reviving her.

Tom Shakespeare

From *The Leap in the Dark*

Everyone knew that Tim was absent-minded, but he had never previously lost a pub. He was forever losing other things: phone, keys, gloves, scarves, woolly hats. Particularly the woolly hats. His grandmother always said that knitting was therapeutic, so more knitting could only be more therapeutic. His mother maintained that it was his head that was woolly, not the headgear. Summer, even a British summer, certainly offered fewer items to mislay. Tim was tall, thin, and his mop of hair (uncontrollable) was the colour of a raven's wing. In later years, it would fade to spun silver. Under the uncontrollable hair, his brain was usually occupied with theoretical physics, or birds, or sometimes the intricate mathematics of Bach fugues. But he kept forgetting things, and his grandmother kept knitting him hats.

Tim was not yet twenty, and he didn't tie knots in a pocket handkerchief, which had been an unfashionable reminder long before the Covid pandemic. Tim had discovered that the best solution for absent-mindedness was to set himself alarms on his mobile phone. Although this strategy too could end in embarrassment. Once, in a first term lecture, the phone had chimed to remind him of his lunchtime dental appointment, and two hundred heads had swivelled in his direction. No one in his year had ever paid him this much attention before. Now he had evinced such curiosity that he felt he had no choice but to leave the lecture theatre immediately. A check-up was definitely required, but he would have preferred it without his physics lecturer scowling at him quite so severely. He resolved to send her a note of apology afterwards, although perhaps he would take the precaution of forging his handwriting. At least it was now the era of anonymous marking. And the Portuguese oral hygienist had been rather insistent.

But at lunchtime on March 12th, the road to which he had found his way back was pub-less. The other houses were just as he'd left them the night before. He'd read that property prices in Norwich were rocketing nearly to London heights. Farrow and Ball paint was popular throughout the Golden Triangle of middle-class Norwich and beyond. But here there was no obvious *Leap in the Dark* signboard creaking in the breeze. One Georgian terraced house was connected to another, with no gaps, and definitely no pubs. Perhaps it was it was just the wrong street, thought Tim. Obviously, he had been more tired than he remembered the night before. He knew he hadn't been drunk. He'd had one coffee and one J2O all evening.

Wondering where he had taken the wrong turn, he tried the next road. The *Leap* wasn't there either. With increasing anxiety, he searched the neighbourhood. It wasn't a district of Norwich that he knew very well, and the streets were higgledy-piggledy. A nearby church chimed the half hour. He felt like a fool, as if he was letting his people down. Failing to find your own place of work looked much like incompetence, even for someone as absent-minded as him.

After an hour of shamefaced searching, he gave up, and slowly walked back to the flat he shared off Earlham Road. He had to admit that he couldn't, for the life of him, find *The Leap in the Dark*. No Joe, no Griet, no Hedwig. He felt mortified. He had liked them! Over the previous ten days or so it felt like they had become his friends. And now it was as if they were gone from his life. But now he had coursework to do.

Aside from his flat mates, Tim did not have a lot of friends. The birding crowd were not unfriendly, but they weren't exactly mates, most of them. And the physics students, four fifths of them males in shapeless hoodies and jeans, seemed to have inherited the grunting gene, but not the one that coded for conversation, let alone companionship.

Within a day or two, his flat-mates stopped taking the piss. And after a month he'd almost forgotten it himself. He'd been paid for his few weeks work. He discovered that the money was going further than he thought, and then the rest of the Lent term went in a whirl. Busy with assignments, he didn't often think back to his capers in *The Leap in the Dark*. Now and then a fragment of a folk-tune, some Irish air or Scotch gig came to him as he was falling asleep or walking home, an elegy for a time where he was beginning to feel that he belonged. He still wanted to find his way back there, if only to say sorry for going astray. And then there was the matter of the hearing aid, and his promise.

An English person's home is their pub, or at least at one time it was, and for good reason. A pub, also variously known as an ale-houses, tavern or inn, is a subdued welcome in an atmosphere suffused with congenial alcohol. A place where you can be with friends, to sit at a table and have a convivial evening of chat and laughter. A place you can go with your best mate, to sit in a corner and glower about the foolishness of the world. Somewhere you can sit with the person of your dreams, and gaze into their eyes, and feel completely insulated from all around you.

Most importantly, a place where you can go on your own and be left to your own devices, where nobody thinks worse of you for having no companions, where it is entirely acceptable to read a book, or even gaze into space while you slowly sip your pint of whatever also is local by way of alcoholic beverage. A pub is everything you want it to be, and nothing forced down your neck, where you remember how closely related brand is to brandishing, where the only acceptable marketing is the little mat under your glass which you slowly tear into shreds as you set everything to rights. A pub is somewhere that has been doing its job for several centuries, and has got rather good at it. Almost by definition, a pub that looks old, is new: too shiny-old, too samey-old, to carpentered and decorated. A pub that looks new, with bits of linoleum and peeling 1970s wallpaper, is un-restored, has not changed, is reassuringly familiarly shabby. And the toilets will always be freezing cold, and there will be a gutter urinal for the gents.

Over the years, many notable things have been started in pubs. Plans for the Boston Tea Party (1773), the world's first steam railway (1825) and the rules of soccer (1832) were all drawn up in pubs, as were the words to Rule Britannia (1740). General George Washington (1783) and Horatio Nelson (1793) said their farewells in pubs. On February 28th, 1953, Francis Crick and James Watson went for lunch in The Eagle on Bene't Street, Cambridge and announced to anyone listening that they had just discovered the secret of life, having worked out the structure of DNA at the Cavendish laboratory just up the street. On June 28th, 1969, the riots that kicked off gay liberation began in The Stonewall Inn, New York.

Ignorant of the cultural history, barely cognizant of the well-known merits of the public house over, say, the student bar, Tim's main ambition that late February morning was just not to freeze. The sky over Norwich was clear and the sun was shining. Although there was barely warmth to the sun beams, the early frost had gone. Dawn came earlier each day, and with it the chorus of songbirds reminding Tim of life continuing and the eternal cycle beginning again. If only the easterly wind were to let up for a bit, you could imagine that the worst of winter was over. What he needed now was a source of radiant heat, rapidly followed by lunch.

Tim was broke, and he required a job. He had never planned to do a temporary job for long. It was impossible to fit in paid work and do a physics degree anyway. Physics tended to be the sort of course you had to be dedicated to. Those who had other interests—girls, politics, beer—tended to be weeded out, and ended up doing easier courses or more applied subjects, like engineering. It was bad enough that Tim played the French horn and was interested in birds. It would have been much better to have been solely motivated by the very early Universe or the Higgs bosun or black holes. The ones who did really well in Physics didn't have outside interests. They thought, ate and slept Physics. Often, even eating and sleeping were optional. These students were almost always male, and a polite observer might have described them as 'on the spectrum'. If they talked at all, it was about where they would go to do their Phds, or a comparison of the available facilities—not the nightlife—in Chicago, Paris and Geneva. People like this did not tend to be good at life, thought Tim, because they shut almost all of it out, not just the nightlife. The nerds weren't even very good at explaining the tough bits of physics. When something comes naturally to you, you don't really understand what is hard about it, which means you cannot easily explain it to someone else.

Tim wanted to be the sort of physicist who knew about things other than physics—like birds, say, or Bach fugues. He harboured the ambition to be able to do more than maintain basic hygiene. He thought cooking for people sounded an attainable goal. More than that, he aspired to talk to the opposite sex in an engaging way, rather than with a muttered "Excuse me," or "Pass the sauce". He wasn't exactly sure that any of these objectives were compatible with being a proper physicist. He had heard of successful physics couples, when two like-minded researchers formed a covalent bond, which meant when attraction and repulsion were equally balanced. He thought he could aspire to achieving that. He had some idea about the chemistry. So far, he hadn't managed more than a flustered "hello", but by the third year, he hoped to have worked his way up to a conversation, after which, who knew what might happen.

Physics was a full-time job in itself. Most mornings he had lectures, and several times each week there was also a practical class in the afternoon. The lecture courses had user-friendly titles such as "An introduction to relativity" and "Astrophysics for beginners", but after the first lecture, the talks became more and more complex and deeply mathematical. Soon, Tim had been told about almost as many fundamental constants as he had fingers and toes: G, the gravitational constant; c, the speed of light, h, the Plank constant; the fine structure constant; the mass of an electron; the Josephson constant; the Rydberg constant . . . on nights when he could not get to sleep, it was easier to list and define constants than to count sheep, which were far less interesting.

The afternoon practical classes were where, week by week he and the others set out to take measurements of physical phenomena, under the direction of a graduate student. Put together, these measurements enabled them to see basic laws of physics in operation. In a way, they were simply recapitulating the history of physics in the twentieth century: the speed of light, relativity. They weren't discovering anything new, that was left to the postgraduates and principal investigators whom they hoped to tag along with.

Tim was very impressed that one of their classes was taken by a female postgrad. It was proof that women could progress in his discipline. He wondered whether she had a boyfriend. Perhaps it was someone in the same lab as her. Maybe she was better than him. He thought he'd like to do postgrad work. But in the meantime, he would have to fit everything in. Juggling a part-time job and the physics course was almost impossible. But as previously observed, Tim needed the money.

That morning, his flat-mate Jesse had bounced out of his room rather exuberantly, and well before 10am. Tim looked at him suspiciously through a cloud of smoke, clutching the jam jar of instant coffee that would serve as his cup until someone had done the washing up.

"Burnt the toast again?" asked Jesse, shutting the kitchen door and opening the back door. Their fire alarm was as over-sensitive as a narcissist on Twitter, and the neighbours had already complained twice that week.

It was possible that Frank, third member of the household, was still sleeping upstairs. Nobody would know, or dared look. He might be there, he might not. That's why Tim though to him as Schrödinger's Flat Mate. On a good day, he slept until the afternoon. Often, he wasn't there at all, because he was sleeping over somewhere. Possibly with a girlfriend after a heavy night at the LCR. Equally likely, in a ditch. Frank had an extraordinary talent for unconsciousness. It was his superpower. Sleeping through a fire alarm was child's play to him. Offering a logical challenge to a flatmate came as second nature.

Tim took a long slurp from his cup/jar. Just as well he liked it black, he thought morosely. They'd run out of milk again, and he was certain it wasn't his turn to go out and buy it. He stared moodily at the garden. Their back yard only loosely merited the word 'garden'. Its main feature was mud. A tree-stump offered some relief to the eye; chunks of bacon rind, and breadcrumbs, and bird food were sprinkled on and around it. Was that a jay? wondered Tim. He peered more closely. Perhaps it was a just a particularly perky crisp packet in the breeze. He definitely needed his glasses.

"It's my birthday!" announced Jesse, putting the kettle on. This explained the exuberance.

"FFS!" said Tim, turning away from the window. "You could have warned us earlier!"

"Why?" asked Jesse, curiously. "Would you have bought me a present?"

"Possibly a card," admitted Tim. There was a Tesco at the service station at the end of the road.

"Not breakfast in bed?" asked Jesse, as he poured boiling water into the mug he'd previously rinsed under a tap.

"Highly unlikely," said Tim, firmly. "But you can have this piece of marmite toast". He held it out. Jesse inspected it. It was extremely charred.

"I'll give it a miss, thanks all the same."

"How old are you, in fact?" asked Tim, after a moment of reflective munching. He knew his flat mate was older than he was. Perhaps philosophy required maturity. Although Jesse was barely more mature in terms of wisdom, and seemed to spend more time on the history of science than philosophy.

"Chronologically, 20" said Jesse, throwing a tea bag in the general direction of the black bag that served as their bin. "Although literally speaking, five."

"How so?" asked Tim, bemused. Five sounded extremely immature.

"Don't you know what day it is?" enquired his flat mate.

"Err, Thursday?"

"The what?"

"Umm, 27th? 28th?" Tim floundered. It definitely wasn't bin day.

"No, clutz! It's February 29th 2024. Leap Year Day! I was born twenty years ago this very day, which makes me a Leapling."

"Come again?"

"Someone born on Leap Year Day is a Leapling."

"Never heard of it . . . "

"Which means," continued Jesse, "given that twenty is divisible by four, that because I have only had five actual birthdays, then I must be five!"

"As Niels Bohr once said," said Tim, not to be outdone, "'you are not thinking. You are just being logical'. Anyway, if you're only five, I should definitely have bought you a Very Hungry Caterpillar cake!"

"You still can" said Jesse, triumphantly.

It was the only birthday cake they stocked in Tesco. They both knew this to be true because they'd bought one at midnight after a freshers' party the previous autumn. The sugar rush had kept them up arguing about Brexit until 2am, and they were sure it was the only explanation for why they each had had a hangover the next day.

Half an hour later, dressed and ready, broadly speaking, for whatever challenges the day might bring, Tim wandered along streets that were almost empty, with his head down, contemplating his physics assignments. He had several problem-based worksheets to complete. Looking up, he was surprised to find himself in an unfamiliar area of town. He knew the town centre should be somewhere ahead of him, if he headed eastwards. Today was the deadline he had set himself for finding a job, which is why he had originally embarked in this direction.

He had started his first year as a student with a reassuringly healthy bank balance. He even bought another pair of jeans (black), and a physics department hoodie (also black). His student loan felt like a windfall from a conveniently deceased relative, and he was briefly generous with himself. He was in the black (fiscally, as well as literally). Still, after the first semester, his rent, the shopping and his course books, he was now almost overdrawn. He'd either have to live on lentils until June, or somehow fit in a job alongside his coursework.

Quarks up and quarks down, quarks strange and quarks charmed, squeezed his job search out of his mind. Fundamental particles were spinning away at the heart of the matter, bound with strange forces, like Tolkien's rings. He mentally admonished himself. He should have been on his way to the temping agency, not dawdling through Norwich's medieval byways while pondering fermions, let alone hypothetical super-partners (his own super partner was certainly entirely hypothetical).

He passed a wall sign recording that one Will Kemp, apparently one of Shakespeare's acting troupe, had Morris-danced all the way from London to Norwich in nine days in 1599. It was that sort of a city. Quirky. Or did he mean quarky?

It was the loud groan that made him look up. It might have been the sigh of someone who had seen everything many times before. Or perhaps a large dog waiting for his breakfast. Only, there was no one there. It could have been the air brakes of an articulated lorry. Only, there wasn't one of those either. Probably just a benign example of East Anglia's many variants on a gale, thought Tim. Around him, the street was empty. There was only a row of higgledy-piggledy houses, and the occasional faded shop-front where, in better days, locals had bought groceries. At the end of the street was a pub, yet another of his adopted city's many hostelries.

At UEA Freshers' Fayre, he had been assured that there were three hundred and sixty-five pubs in Norwich. According to the local saying, a pub for every day of the year was leavened by a church for every Sunday. Tim felt this only proved that the good burghers and laboring people of Norwich had been historically rather keener on things of the malt than things of the spirit. It was still the case. Tim had visited a few of the city's hostelries, sampling the fine East Anglian ales of Mr Greene and Mr King and Mr Woodforde and the Adnams brothers on the notorious theoretical physics undergrad pub crawls. But this tavern was new to him.

He took a few steps towards it. An old, brick building that matched its neighbours, probably Georgian, he imagined, with only the faded sign swinging in the breeze that showed that it was still a pub. It must have been the creak of the pintles which he'd just heard. He looked up at the faded and peeling pub sign, which showed two people holding hands and jumping over a crescent moon, and saw it also bore a name: *The Leap In the Dark*.

As he gazed at the signboard, trying to understand what it could be depicting, a cellar hatch opened, first with a creak, and then with a crash. A head popped through at pavement level and looked up and down the street, as if he were a character making his entrance upon Shakespeare's Globe, to which his parents had taken Tim. Despite bushy, wiry hair at the back and sides, the top of the head was quite bald. It could have been a clown's head, had it not been for the rather magnificent beard, above which two beady brown eyes were squinting in the February sunshine. All very Falstaffian, not least the warm and richly honied voice that now issued from a mouth that presumably lurked behind the beard:

"Seen a dray?"

It took Timothy a moment to realize that the man was asking him. And a moment longer to remember that a dray was the old name for a brewery lorry.

"No. Sorry," he said, "Only just turned the corner myself."

There was a nod from the foot-level Falstaff.

"Probably got lost."

The head was now followed by broad shoulders, as two big hands hauled out the rest of the body, so that in a second or two, a man sat perched on the edge of the opening. The usual complement of legs and arms and head, a man barely out of breath, and now drawing a tobacco pouch from the pocket of his leather apron. He rolled himself a cigarette in one practiced movement, and eyed Timothy up and down.

"You need a job."

Tim started, looked round to check there was no one else there. The man from the pub was talking to him. It was as if he had read his mind . . .

"I do, yes . . . "

"Got one here, if you like. If it's temporary you're looking for . . . "

" . . . End of the academic year coming up, last of the student loan and, well, my parents aren't really . . . I need something temporary. Oh sorry?"

Tim had been too busy talking to notice that the bearded man had interjected.

"Done bar work before?" The man with the nut-brown face, now puffing away happily on his cigarette, winked at Timothy in a rather disconcerting way.

"Yes. I've been a waiter, glass collector, cinema usher," Tim replied. "Been behind the bar too. All temporary."

Tim did not feel it sensible to disclose that this last assignment had been rather briefer than he had hoped, owing to misunderstandings over operating the cash register. Mental arithmetic was a doddle, compared to managing the intricacies of modern machinery.

"Start at midday, finish going on midnight," said the publican. "Twelve hours a day with breaks. One hundred pound, cash in your hand. Does that suit? Is that enough these days?"

"Oh! Yes. That sounds great. One hundred would be ideal . . . If you can."

"Fine". The man thrust out a brawny arm, the blue of fading tattoos disappearing under his rolled-up shirtsleeves.

"Joe," he announced.

Timothy leaned down and grasped the proffered hand.

"Timothy. Usually known as Tim".

"If I can call Time, I can call Tim" said Joe. "Now come on in."

Matthew Tomkinson

Cathedral of Greebles

SETTINGS	The revolving door of the brain; the prop shop of the cranium; the corporate archive of Broca's area; the auction house of cortical memory; the recycling depot with its mishmash of abject mysteries; the vast stash-house of backdrops; the vaster burning city; an empty dance hall; a collapsing circus tent; the disaster area not yet a photo, the damage still potential light.
DIRECTOR	The mind motored by its fear of failure.
STAGE MANAGER	The cardboard cop with his arms folded.
CHARACTERS	The male stripper in the big cage; the reptile in the smaller cage; the speed-walker who could never leave the house without humming; a government official who is always late for his meetings; the sad dad who does dollar-bill magic; some penitents seated on the pew-ends of the psyche; the protruding eyes of Panic Pete.
PROPS	The hairy basketball; the hairless basketball; the tree whose needles do not accord with the story they're in; the sunburned skin of a whale's carcass; the jar that holds the wrestler's sweat; a coronal of calla lilies; a fake cake; a real sword; a fossil of the brontosaur; a leech clinging to the ankle of a mermaid; a silent cellphone in the pocket of a passed-out picnicker; a licence plate from a famous car chase; a first-draft screenplay stolen from set; mandalas of dust on a panel of glass; the stem and stamen of a polyester flag; the pressure-vessel of a spray can in your hand; the dried-up bark of far-off history; a hand-painted animation cell extracted from your racing thoughts, signed; sun-bleached barnacles on the hull of time.
COSTUMES	Death mask of an ex-custodian; a helmet of fruit leathers sourced from the break room; a beard of flies born within the exit sign.
LIGHTING	The settling spores of the larch buds breaking; a fan-powered flame of silk.
SOUND DESIGN	The din of stone-burnished pots; bats flapping in a roost; the vocal fry of geiger counters
MUSICAL NUMBERS	<u>ACT I</u> "A Dog's Love Is More Acceptable to the World" "Heat Eats the Puddles, and the Pictures in Them" "Quit Trying to Intone the Obvious with Your Dithyrambs" "We Are the Ungrounded, the Voltages of Heaven in Our Uncombable Hair" "Cigar Smoke (Follows Me Around)" <u>ACT II</u> "The Neighbour's Donkey Can Work the Lighthouse Lever" "The Snail Pushes Its Shell toward the Mud It Loves" "A Bug Wedges Itself Between Imperfections" "The Recent Past Is an Arsonist in Your Yard" "There's A New Type of Wood That Can't Be Carved"
CAST	A sleeping man in a sleeping bag in a sleeping car on a sleeper train that sleeps through one morning into the next morning.
UNDERSTUDIES	A triangle of sharks.
DANCERS	A salt-clump of saltimbanques; the hollow colonies of the volvox.
CHOREOGRAPHER	A miked-up hyena in the motorcade.
SPECIAL THANKS	To the memory of our Anonymous Donor, who I am sad to say I never met.
RUNTIME	5 hours
INTERMISSION	15 minutes

Tomoé Hill

The Choreography of Ruin

That which I sow, that which I reap.
What grows without, what grows within.

Back and forth like asynchronous pendulums, a group of dancers come together, then fall apart. The arms in a Pina Bausch work twist and freeze, a mirror to dead and dying Puglian groves where the olive trees, once solid and eternally ancient, grow no more but remain in ruin, as far as the eye can see. Blighted, taken over from the inside. *A distortion of the womb*. Wilhelm Flusser says 'to plant means to . . . force nature to become unnatural'. To take this out of its context still retains something of the original: this distortion exists in what was the field of my body. This blight is a planting where there had been none. What of the agriculture of the disrupted body? This is my harvest now, both seen and unseen: the fallow field, the consumed tree. I am the stripped limb contorted, a cavity frozen in its Bausch-like movements. I am now the choreography of ruin.

Not long ago there was a single dancer, a single growth. Alone, it reached and swayed to an invisible song. Flusser again: 'the gesture of planting is . . . the overture to the gesture of waiting'. Eventually joined by its others, it began to reshape the field that had intentionally grown nothing. Unnatural nature is still a flourishing: rot, decay, ruin all being harvests of a sort, the fruition of destruction. The body in itself is not evil. When Flusser speaks of the gesture of destroying, again I cannot help but place it within a context of what goes on inside of me. My body and I are now silently combative: I will it; it refuses to heed. I wish it to stop its intrusive process, but it continues with a determination which leaves me in near-admiration. 'Destruction . . . negates not just the way the object is but the object itself'. It is beautiful in its focus, this goal of totality.

I am being changed by a body which has interpreted my inaction, my non-possession of a secret space as an abandonment. It is a destruction of nothing, but the taking over of possibility. More dancers, more distortion, reminding me from time to time of its intention in erratic gestures: this watching of time for a thing which does not appear, the holding back and release of red. -*rhage*,'to burst forth, to break'. -rhage, rage, the sea (the wine-dark sea), the womb, swaying limbs, the dances of growth and destruction. It is the essence of purpose. Since seeing those olive trees through a moving car's window—giving the impression of the movement of mourners, only aware of their grief—I watch videos of Bausch's works: *Orpheus and Eurydice*, *Àgua*, *The Rite of Spring*, the movements of the dancers the quintessence of emotion. Whether lone or in groups, bodies translated the *abstractness* of the body—its cohesion and division—channelling sense and feeling through their very flesh, conduits of the internal. I reread Robert Aickman's 'Ringing the Changes', in which the dead rise up and dance, the living, both willing and unwilling, swept up in a frenzied mass. Life and death, and the movements which are the distillation of them.

The body is not evil, I tell myself. The body requires purpose. I have not fulfilled it and so it has reclaimed it for its own. This takeover, possession, abduction, however you want to phrase it, fascinates me as much as one can be fascinated by the symptoms of a change which foreshadows . . . what? Not death, which is our inevitability. My change is a crossroads, and I hold a clock which tells no time, has not yet stopped. In Aickman's 'The Wine-Dark Sea', the magical island itself lives. Its character's folly is that of never regarding as such it in the first place, thereby losing paradise once again. Paradise is a choice wherein the inhabitant must recognise they are inhabited as much as they inhabit. I have forgotten that the body is the island. Like Grigg, I am cast away but remain attached dream-like, by loss, never to return.

Gaston Bachelard, in response to Henri Michaux's poem 'L'espace aux ombres' (Shade-Haunted Space) in *The Poetics of Space*, says 'intimate space loses its clarity, while exterior space loses its void, void being the raw material of possibility of being. We are banished from the realm of possibility'. One of the lines of this poem which Bachelard refers to is 'space, but you cannot even conceive the horrible inside-outside that real space is'. And when he (Bachelard) later writes, 'in this ambiguous space, the mind has lost its geometrical homeland and the spirit is drifting', more than ever it seems this new loss is being reformed, recalculated by a body intent on defining a meaning and drawing boundaries for itself, outside of my presumptions of use or non-use. Where the olive trees have presumed their possibility, bearing fruit, something now enters and supplants both its space and meaning. So it is within me.

In Pina Bausch's 2007 Kyoto Prize speech, it is the unknown and the sensorial which emerges as the great connections of the elements within her life. Alongside what one does when presented with the unknown via the effects of war, of not knowing a language, of being in a strange new place, of needing to create and communicate in alternate ways in order to find a solution, she describes her memories as pictures, more often than not with a deep sensory description. A recollection of having little money due to saving in order to remain in New York has a surprising contrast. She lives on the fat of a mix of ice cream, buttermilk, lemons, and sugar, but grows thinner. She notes the clarity which comes from this juxtaposition: 'I paid more and more attention to the voice within me. To my movement . . . a transformation was taking place. Not only with my body'. When one is limited in any way, but especially in one which restricts the body, a focus shapes itself from what is absent. This is the clarity of necessity: something like hunger or illness sharpens an outlook, even temporarily.

Why was it, I wonder, that those olive groves should so immediately—viscerally—remind me of what was happening inside of me? Or why the image of Pina's dancers should appear? In Greece, I was struck by their groves: as healthy as the others were ill. Their beauty mattered little, the richness of their oil only caused me to give more thought to their unfruitful siblings. It was the twisted, greying trunks now distorting the landscape which clung to my mind, the external representation my condition. Susan Stewart writes of ruins, 'a ruin confuses the interior with the exterior . . . as it also shows the interrelatedness of these aspects of perception'. So long had I considered these two aspects of myself as unrelated despite having had other issues that it felt as though I was facing an obsolete self. Part of me was history in that this new change was irreversible, and though it is possible to be stopped, there is no sense of time. To stop will mean yet another kind of ruin, where destruction is no longer active but I am left like those ancient olives, a remainder and reminder of nature's unnatural whims.

Is there clarity then, a focus left in this inside-out space which no longer belongs to me? What I desire is akin to an extension. An extended arm or leg reaching towards the infinite, the line which represents continuation. To go on as the trees have not, to become an essence out of chaos, spare and precise, which my exterior and interior come to understand is its transformation. The agriculture of the disrupted body is a metamorphosis, an alchemical change. Women to trees, lead into gold. Where there was once absence and intrusion, we now cultivate movements from corporeal memories lasting as long as the clocks choose to go on.

Polly Atkin

Undiagnosing Dorothy

Posthumous diagnosis is by its very nature problematic. The ethics of diagnosing the dead are questionable, and the practicalities unfeasible. More often than not, there is no body to examine, no physical record of disease or disorder. Where there is a body, and it can be examined, it may not retain any useful evidence. Most conditions cannot be diagnosed from bones alone. Where there is no body, retrospective diagnosis relies on textual records, often letters and diaries, which may be missing key elements of the story, or worse, represent hearsay and gossip that has little to do with what the person in question actually experienced.

I know from my own experience how much diagnosis depends on asking the right questions, and how much knowing which questions to ask, and how useful the answers will be, depends on what information is available. In my case, it took a lifetime of asking the wrong questions, or the right questions with partial information, before my primary diagnoses were found, almost incidentally. It took one person to ask a simple question that hadn't been asked before, to kick off a chain reaction which led to the right tests, which lead to more questions, which lead to more answers. It was luck or chance that one of the specialists I was sent to for one genetic condition asked very thorough questions and uncovered the other genetic condition. Previous blood results that suggested it might be present had been discounted, because of partial information, a lack of understanding, a presumption that younger women did not develop this particular condition. Every step from the age of two till thirty-four that delayed my diagnoses was like this—someone looked at evidence and either misfiled it or dis- counted it—based on their own assumptions. This is not what I want to do with Dorothy. I want to undiagnose Dorothy, not to diagnose her. I want to ask the right questions, and to gather as much evidence as there is available. But I know two things: I have my own biases which will determine both my questions and how I interpret the answers I find, and I do not have all the information.

Lack of information and diagnostic bias has determined the diagnoses lain on Dorothy by previous biographers and commentators. Dorothy has been diagnosed with many things by many people, some of them agreeing with each other, some of them not.

The mysteriousness of Dorothy's illness has drawn attention from doctors over the years, who have attempted to diagnose her as a cold case from letters and journals entries. In the *Journal of the Royal Society of Medicine* in 1998 John Price theorises that her cognitive and mobility changes were caused by thiamin deficiency, caused by her 'vomiting and decreased food intake' during the crisis of December 1832, which developed into Wernicke-Korsakoff Syndrome. Wernicke-Korsakoff Syndrome is characterised by mental confusion, vision changes, and loss of muscle coordination. It could explain some of Dorothy's symptoms, but like so many attempts to diagnose her, it does not quite seem to fit. Ironically, Price recognises the problems inherent in trying to diagnose long deceased patients from partial descriptions, comparing it to archaeology, where the 'evidence is likely to be incomplete or even fragmentary', but argues that it is possible to 'assemble the historical fragments so as to produce a recognisable whole.' In archaeology, he says, you can learn enough to tell whether shards of pottery are a cup, or a saucer. Like many diagnosticians of Dorothy, Price has only looked at the published letters, alongside Gittings and Manton's biography, as his evidence base. I fear, to use his analogy, he may have confused cup and saucer after all.

In the introduction to her 1971 edition of Dorothy's journals Mary Moorman writes in passing that Dorothy was suffering from untreated gallstones which caused progressive arterio-sclerosis, which in turn affected her brain. Gallstone disease is known to often co-exist with coronary artery atherosclerotic disease, and studies in the last decade have sought to confirm this link.

Arteriosclerosis—known more widely now as atherosclerosis—is a condition in which plaque builds up in arteries, restricting oxygen access to organs and potentially causing blood clots, angina, heart attacks and strokes. This is a compel- ling idea and could explain how the acute episodes of the first half of the 1830s come to change the way Dorothy thinks and acts. A stroke or blood clots could indeed account for some of Dorothy's symptoms after her acute attacks—the swelling, discolouration and weakness of her legs, her confusion—and for her cognitive changes after the crisis of 1835. I'm not convinced Gallstone Disease fits the full range of Dorothy's bowel symptoms as collected in this chapter, but I do think the idea that something happened during those crises that affected her brain, something that could be vascular in nature, stands up. Importantly, Moorman was firm in asserting Dorothy's 'illness had purely physical causes, and if she had lived in our own age could have been treated'. She found 'the notion put about recently, that D.W.'s mind was affected by emotional distress, is not tenable.' Moorman stands out as one of the few commentators who has not identified Dorothy's illness as psychological in some or all parts. Gallstones and arteriosclerosis is the diagnosis Carl Ketchum repeats in his introduction to Dorothy's *Rydal Journals* in 1974. Robert Gittings and Jo Manton's 1985 biography agrees that gall bladder disease is responsible for Dorothy's first acute illness in 1829, but suggests that her cognitive changers are unconnected.They consulted an expert in age-related illnesses, who suggested 'we try too much to link all her illnesses', and that her dementia had nothing to do with her painful bilious attacks. The expert concluded she had pre-senile dementia. Dorothy managed to live an unusually long time with dementia, he theorised, because of the 'loving care' provided to her. It is useful to be reminded that not every symptom is connected, but the cognitive changes occur after a physical crisis, so the idea they could be coincidental seems less likely. In her 1988 book *Dorothy Wordsworth, Writer*, Pamela Woof agrees that Dorothy was 'suffering probably from what is now known as pre-senile dementia'. This diagnosis of pre-senile dementia has stuck for many, partly because of Woof's incredible expertise when it comes to Dorothy, partly because of the popular readability of Gittings and Manton's thorough *Life*.

Certainly, there are some elements of her conditions that could suggest dementia. From 1835 onwards her short-term memory seems to be impacted by her condition, yet her memory of the past seems compellingly present. In December 1837, after Elizabeth Rawson's death, William writes to Edward Ferguson that Dorothy 'talks much of Halifax and early connections there; nothing indeed seems to employ her thoughts so much.' (WW to Edward Ferguson, December 30, 1837). Evidence for dementia has also been found in Mary and William's numerous accounts of Dorothy's 'childishness' during her acute illness, and the years that follow. She becomes, Mary writes, party to 'ungovernable passions'. In other words, she wants to do what she wants to do. Visitors to Rydal Mount in her later years report on how remarkable it is that with her 'enfeebled mind' Dorothy can recite the poems of Coleridge and repeat stories of their youth. It is clear how be read as indicating dementia, but it also only seems to me to be part of the story of Dorothy's illness, and not to explain it all. Despite apparent memory loss, and dwelling on the past, Dorothy seems to shift in and out of the present moment over her last twenty years. Although she does not write a lot during this time, she does write and recite poems and she does write some short letters. Most importantly, whatever has happened to her is not obviously progressive. Something happens in the last crisis in 1835, which changes her cognitive function for the rest of her life. But from that time on, there is no further progression, just daily fluctuations. More recently, Lucy Newlyn has combined theories to conclude that 'Dorothy's later years [. . .] were blighted by arteriosclerosis and dementia.' It seems unlikely Dorothy could have lived with fluctuating cognitive function but have had stable health for twenty years if this were her diagnosis, no matter how much loving care she was given.

This lack of an immediate, simple explanation for Dorothy's memory and mood changes has led other scholars to discount a physical cause at all, as Moorman indicated, and assume the illness is emotional or psychogenic in some way. In this they are harking back, wittingly or unwittingly, to those Victorian commentors who believed she became ill through thinking too much, or too little, of herself. Francis Wilson diagnosed Dorothy with depressive pseudodementia, caused somehow by a *very* delayed response to no longer being the centre of William's life after his marriage. Wilson realised that Dorothy's disease progression and length does not map easily onto a diagnosis of organic dementia. It also does not map well onto pseudodementia, which is a contested diagnosis at the best of times. Even when her cognitive function is most disrupted, she has highly emotional responses to stimuli, making jokes, weeping at flowers, and becoming angry when refused something she wants, none of which fit with this functional dementia-like condition, sec- ondary to depression, and most often recorded as a side-effect of medication. Susan Levin, despite her ground-breaking work in collecting Dorothy's poems, and careful, thoughtful, reading of her letters and journals, similarly assumes that the mysteriously fluctuating nature of Dorothy's illness means it can only be explained by 'feminine psychology'. As an invalid, Levin argues, Dorothy can do as she wants, living 'authentically' as herself, 'both the old Dorothy whom everyone knows and loves and the aggressively unacceptable crazy lady.'

The idea illness offers a 'release' to Dorothy does not stand up to much scrutiny, though it repeats charges made a billion times against a billion sick women: that we are not *really* sick, just pretending, to get our own way. This psychologising always presupposes there is more to gain than there is to lose from life in the sickroom. It confuses the need all newly disabled people have to adjust to their situation and find ways to experience pleasure and joy in their changed life, and that changed life being a choice they have made towards happiness. Dorothy, it is true, finds solace in her illness, but it is clear it is not her choice. She finds solace despite her illness, not because of it. It also repeats another harm committed repeatedly against the mysteriously sick, and sick women in particular: to assume that since the cause and name of an illness it not known, the illness does not have a physical basis. It happens often in medical con- texts, but it seems particularly strange to me that scholars can admire a writer or an artist from the past so much that they will spend their life dedicated to their work, but also distrust them to the point of disbelieving their own witness of their own life. Having said that, Dorothy's description of her own condition cannot always be taken entirely at face value, or as complete. There are three kinds of records we have of her illness in her own words: her poems, her letters, and her journals. The *Rydal Journals*—not written to be shared in the same way as her earlier journals were—are the most intimate of these records, and the least censored (by her own hand, at least). Her poems are made artfully, and though they reveal her own feelings about her situation, they also are formed through what she wants to feel about her situation, and what she wants to tell others. They are written to be read and shared. They are designed as communication.

In her letters, even as her condition progresses, she is very aware of her audience and their expectations. They often have a cheerful, self-deprecating tone, especially when describing the seriousness of her condition. She never wants her correspondents to worry unnecessarily. For instance, in 1830 she describes herself to her god-daughter Elizabeth Hutchinson as both old and 'infirm', but she does so to point out how entertaining her visit will be, as a 'lively companion and useful help' (DW to Elizabeth Hutchinson, July 16, 1830). I know I self-censor my words when I tell others how I am. There are some friends I am more open with than others, but if a future archivist were to search for records of my illness, they would not find the worst of my experiences. Sometimes, they are beyond words. Sometimes I will repeat them only in person, the words floating off, ephemeral, reduced to half a sentence or an aside. Sometimes I make notes for myself, in case I need them later, but even those will not reflect the whole truth. There is so much daily body horror that goes unrecorded.

This is what I see when I am faced with the unwritten and fragmented portions of Dorothy's life: what is impossible to write down.

(From *Recovering Dorothy*, Saraband Books, 2021)

Jesi Bender

From Kinderkrankenhaus

ACT I

Scene 2

{lights rise}

Interior, main hall of das Kinderkrankenhaus.

Grey. The hospital is grey. Full of grey beds and grey floors and grey walls. Grey doors with silver handles that glint like a distant freedom. It has grey wiring that cuts a pattern of diamonds in its few windows. Grey: cups, pills, and the paddles of horse-hair brushes. Only grey water runs from its oxidized faucets. The people inside too. Grey.

The wall opposite the the audience is lined with bunk beds. In the exact center of the grey stone wall, there is a small place where the stones have fallen, creating a small cavern. Above the entry a ∑ has been carved.

All children inside wear a grey tunic that is sealed in the back with a series of ties. Depending on how old the patient is, it falls anywhere between mid-calf all the way down to the ankle. On a few, it skims the floor. Their hair is cut identically as well, in a bob no longer than the bottom of their earlobes. At the midpoint of their skull, the hair is parted and fringe is cut in the front so that it falls right above the eyebrows. Unless the patient has coarse hair. In that case, the nurses shave the whole head clean. Even the eyebrows. Not the only extra abuse patients see for standing out, intentionally or not.

The children are playing. Or doing whatever activities we call play, no matter how silly or serious they may be. The children are.

Gnome enters, led by Dr. Schmetterling (the Doctor's hand on Gnome's shoulder). Stabat Mater.

After a pause to look around, Dr. Schmetterling: "Well, what do you think of your new home?"

Gnome: "It looks like the inside of a rock."

Dr. Schmetterling: "Well . . . that's where you can find a diamond, isn't it?"

the Shadow, rocking in place: "Die man, die man, die man, die man, die man, die man, die man, die man, die man, die man, die man, die man, die man, die—"

Nix: "And fossils, and oil, and minerals, and geodes, and endoliths—"

Dr. Schmetterling: "Yes, children, yes. Enough. Peace please. Come now, quietly, and gather around. Meet our new friend."

Most of the children gather in a circle around Gnome with Doctor Schmetterling at the apex. A few children remain standing where they were before, though some of them are less engaged with their activity.

Dr. Schmetterling: "Well, what should we call this one, Eros?"

Eros, patting Gnome on the head three times: "Gnome. I think. Funny red. Clever red. I think."

Dr. Schmetterling: "Yes, I agree. Gnome. Another little gnome living inside this rock. [leaning down over Gnome] You will be called Gnome from now on."

Gnome : "'Til when?"

Dr. Schmetterling, starting to move down the row of beds: "As long as you're here, [tapping a bunk] this is your place. Right here."

Gnome: "Where? Where?"

Dr. Schmetterling exits without looking back. The children disperse back to their activities, except for Cinders. Periodically, a child lets out a momentary shriek or extended single-note hum.

Cinders: "Das Kinderkrankenhaus."

Word appears [KINDERKRANKENHAUS].

Gnome: "What?"

Cinders: "That's here. Kin-der-kran-ken-haus. It's German."

Gnome, puzzled: "German?"

Cinders: "The name is German. The Germans love compound words."

Gnome: "What is that?"

Cinders: "Words made of more words. Words made of more than just one word."

Gnome: "Like a sentence?"

Cinders: "No."

Gnome: "So, words with more than one meaning?"

Cinders: "No—I mean, like butterfly is made of the word butter and the word fly. Kinderkrankenhaus is three words. [pointing to each part] Kinder meaning children, kranken meaning suffering, and haus meaning . . . house."

Gnome: "Childrensufferinghouse."

Cinders: "Yes, a hospital—for sick kids." Gnome: "Why are we in a hospital?"

Cinders: "Because we're sick, of course. Terribly, terribly sick."

Gnome: "What's wrong with us?"

Cinders: "All sorts of things. Bright, gleaming things."

Gnome, reading: "Kinder crank in hows."

Cinders: "No, *kinder*. Kin. Derrr."

Gnome, sitting on the bunk: "Okay."

Cinders, coming closer: "Don't worry, Gnome. There's always a cure. You just have to want to find it."

Gnome, rolling on their side: "I'm not Gnome."

Cinders, laughs: "You are now. The doctor says so."

Cinders wanders away.

Gnome tosses and turns in the bunk, increasingly agitated. Finally, Gnome stands and says: "How can you cure something you cannot see? Isn't everything made visible through me?"

No one answers. Gnome approaches the Shadow, who is flapping their hands sporadically in front of their body.

Gnome: "What are you doing? Fighting invisible insides?"

Eros: "the Shadow. Don't talk much. No. Mmm."

Gnome: "No one can give me any answers around here."

Eros: "No, don't you know. Know-mmm?"

Gnome: "What makes you think I know anything?"

Eros: "What makes you think? I do."

Gnome, turning to other children: "Do you? Do any of you?"

Nix: "I do. I know any thing. It comes from chaos. Ex nihilo. Genesis. Creation. Procreation. Created from nothing . . ."

Gnome: "How can you make something from nothing?"

Cinders: "You take it in your hands. And you give it a name."

Gnome sits on the ground, starts to cry.

Eros: "Gnome, no. Know no mmm."

Cinders: "Why are you crying?"

Gnome: "I don't like it here."

Eros: "No. One does."

Gnome: "I want to go home."

Nix: "Home is where the heart is."

Gnome: "Where are my parents? Where are all the adults? I don't even know why I'm here. No one told me nothing."

Nix: "Oh, to be here, you must be really ill. Infirm. An epidemic nowadays. Sick, sick children."

Gnome: "How do you know?"

Nix: "That's what they [pointing to the only door] say. The doctors and soldiers and teachers and parents and people with official letters that give us our official names."

Gnome: "What are your official names?"

Nix: "Oh, in here, we are given many names. I am Nix, that is the Shadow, and Cinders. And that is Eros."

Gnome; "Are you saying errors?"

Cinders: "Eros. Air-*Rohs*."

Gnome, pointing to the door: "And they gave you those names?"

Nix: "Oh, no, there is a funny story behind each appellation. Nicknames. Or sobriquets. Or cognomen. Cog-no-men. Cog-gnome-n."

Word appears {COGNOMEN (together-name)}

"A name is how we gnomen, know men."

Cinders, interrupting: "You will have to figure it out or else you'll end up in the Loch."

Gnome: "What?"

Cinders: "Figure out why you're here."

Gnome: "No, what's the Lock?"

Eros: "Oh no, it is a place outside some. Where we don't know, Gnome. Mmm—no know mmm—maybe. Or . . ."

Nix: "We don't know what it means when the Doctor says it's where the disease ceases to be."

Gnome: "So you don't know. But you're still afraid of it."

Cinders: "They're afraid *because* they don't know."

Eros: "You are. Too!"

Cinders: "No, I'm not!"

Nix, quietly: "The children that go there never come back."

Gnome: "Sounds like the kids who don't have to come here. Kids that live without an official name. It sounds like that's where we want to be."

The other children are silent.

Gnome: "If you don't know something's wrong, then couldn't it be alright?"

The Shadow: "All right, all right, all right, all right, all right, [illegible]."

Cinders: "Are you talking about yourself or the Loch?"

Gnome: "How can I ask about something I didn't know existed?"

Cinders: "Well, you do now."

Gnome: "You guys should give up on these goofy names. They're ridiculous. What are your real names?"

Eros: "Oh, Gnome, these. Names have real meaning."

Gnome: "You can't become whatever someone labels you. That name is not a part of you, like your nose."

Nix, slightly desperate: "Oh, no, yes, they are. Eros is right. The name becomes you. No misnomer. No mis-no-more. Miss-gnome-her."

Cinders: "Gnome, don't confuse Nix. We live within a narrow language. Names are everywhere but meaning is mall-able."

Nix: "Malleable! You mean malleable."

Cinders: "Malleable."

Nix, wandering away: "Malleable. Male-he-able. Mmm-ale-e-al. Mallet. Malicious . . ."

Gnome: "No, don't go Nix. [Nix continues off stage] I wanted to ask about the stories behind your names. Are they really funny?"

Cinders: "Depends on what you think is funny."

They stand in silence for a moment, not knowing what to say.

Gnome: "I'm sorry."

Cinders, shrugging: "You don't have to be sorry with me."

Gnome: "No, I just meant in general."

Cinders shrugs again.

Gnome: "Just trying to understand what's going on."

Cinders: "You will have to meet with Doctor Schmetterling soon. There is a personal session for each patient on their second day here. Maybe you'll listen when the Doctor gives you an answer."

Cinders walk away.

Gnome walks to a bed and lays down.

{curtain falls}

(From *Kinderkrankenhaus*, Sagging Meniscus, 2021)

Harry Parker

Dreams of a Broken Body

I open my eyes to the ward. The soundtrack is back: the low hum of machines, the shuffle of a nurse, a monitor chiming on the other side of the ICU. I inch my head around. Curtains are drawn around the bay and the lights are dimmed. The middle of the night. I lie and stare at the wall and become aware of my body. A roll call of body parts checking in. It's too painful and strange to be me—I am dislocated from this broken flesh. My nerves have been shocked by explosives, and everything below the neck is fizzing. There is a whirring also: the analgesia dulling the pain, retuning its frequency so it is just white noise. I feel for my legs along the map of synapses I've known a lifetime, but now my legs are distant, shimmering in a kind of hot furnace beyond my leaden arms and aching back and through the sharpness of lesions and bruising and the fizzing white noise blossoms into pain.

I recoil from it and press the PCA button; it drones and pushes morphine into my central line and after a while I am unconscious.

During those first weeks the shock and drugs and countless surgeries distorted everything. Dreams crossed into waking, so nothing felt real. My imagination seemed to be protecting me from what had happened, walking me around the ward so I could look back at the bed and my body in it, or transport- ing me to places I knew from childhood: to dreams of home, of schools, of the town centre where I was first given the freedom to go shopping on my own—walks from my youth that felt more real than the medicalised world I'd woken to. It was as if my imagination had kicked into overdrive, emerg- ing to take the reins and guide me through the trauma and strangeness—to help me accept a body I knew was mine, but which was full of pain and attached to the wall of a hospital by pipes and wires. And broken. The left leg gone below the knee, the right halfway down the thigh.

I've fumbled around for the memory: that moment I gasped wide-eyed with the realisation that I had lost my legs. I can't find it. No appalling shock of a doctor or family member breaking the news to me. Instead there are many wakings—from deep comfortable sleep, from anaesthetic oblivion, from dreams horrible and brilliantly surreal—each one eroding a little more of my old self, making way for the new one that was forming.

Each year, as 18 July approaches, I think again of how my life has changed. I've heard American military veterans call it a 're-birthday' and celebrate their second lives. I did mark the day in the first year. I had a load of friends round to my flat and had a barbecue. Just a party, no speech or cake, and most people didn't let on that they knew the significance of the date. As the years have passed, I've done less: a night in the pub or a raised glass over dinner. And last year I received a text at lunchtime from a friend telling me to *have a good one* and it took me a few seconds to realise what he was talking about.

The moments of stepping on an improvised explosive device (IeD) are seared into my memory—they seem as perfectly formed as the day it happened: unforgettable, yet probably as unreliable as any of my memories, altered and embellished with each re-remembering. I don't think about it much any more. It's been ten years, and too many experiences are stacked between that day and now. My dreams are different. In sleep, I don't see myself with or without legs, I simply see me. And the daydreams of that broken body lying in hospital have changed too: it is neither what I hoped for, nor what I feared—it is normal. A loss grieved for and accepted. I am not a victim, unable to walk, nor am I entirely freed from my disability. And while some horizons have contracted, others have expanded. Now, if I was offered the chance to rewind, to never have stepped on a bomb, not only would I refuse, I'd actually be terrified of losing this new part of my life. It would be to change my identity, to erase all those experiences, both good and bad, that make me who I am.

It is 18 July again. I am reminded this year by the date on the appointment letter from the limb-fitting centre (my microprocessor knee needs a service). I'm late. It's been a hard night. Our two children have taken turns being awake—another cold—and now my daughter is refusing to get dressed. I pull on my legs while discussing with my partner who will do the nursery pick-up. It is automatic: roll the liners over my stumps and click into the sockets, no novelty, no flinching—a muscle memory strengthened over ten years. Then I put in my contact lenses. The first goes in routinely but my eye flinches around the second lens, flattening it against my finger. I try prodding it in again. It falls on the floor.

In my early thirties I started wearing glasses. I hated the way they felt and the barrier they threw in front of the world, so I tried contacts. 'Only a few hours each day to begin with,' the optician had said, 'Let your eyes get used to them. Let your tolerance build up. And take them out in the evenings, so your eyes can rest.'

'Like learning to use prosthetic legs,' I replied, but he didn't understand.

My half-dressed daughter is banging the shower door open and closed. It's a spaceship and she's going to the Moon. She wants me to come too, but I'm trying to find the lens. There it is. I peel it off the floor, clean it in my mouth, then push it in. My eye waters with pain as I persuade her out of the spaceship and downstairs. I need to find my leg's remote control for the appointment. Through the blur of tears I see it in the key pot, then apologise for the breakfast-time chaos I've abandoned my partner to and leave.

During the drive to the Central London hospital I keep rolling my finger over my eyeball, trying to dislodge whatever is behind my contact lens. I'm pretty sure I've scratched my cornea now. I crane upwards to the rear-view mirror. My eye is bloodshot and closing around the irritation. It's distracting and hard to drive, so I pinch out the lens and flick it away. I will spend the rest of the day with half the world drawn in a misty haze. For once my legs aren't the most annoying med- tech I use.

I'm stuck in traffic and look through the myopic blur at the people on the pavements. The school-bound children are running and jumping onto the brick edging of a flowerbed, bouncing into each other and laughing. They fizz about like loose atoms among the older pedestrians. I notice almost all the adults making their way down the street have a slight limp, an asymmetry to their gait or glasses, or one shoulder lower than the other. Further on there is a man on a mobility scooter. Bodies losing the suppleness of youth, and ageing.

I look for the technologies used to delay, rebuild or replace these losses of youth. How many of them have popped a pill this morning for an illness or pain, or to enhance their diet, mood or intellect? A woman is shuffling past my car now, rotating her waist around a walking stick. Hip transplant probably, or on the waiting list for one. There's a woman in a trouser suit hurrying through the crowd. I imagine a pacemaker keeping her heart in time. The children are gone, skidding around the corner, school bags wheeling.

A bus stops beside me. I look at a teenager sitting on the bottom deck. His neck is bent to a phone, his shoulders hunch to it, white pods in his ears. suspended in his own reality.

Being an amputee in the twenty-first century doesn't make me an outlier; we are all hybrid. And we all suffer losses. For some it is the loss of youth; for others it will be more profound. The possibilities to replace that loss—to merge human and machine—are greater than ever before. Artificial hips and knees are prolonging mobility, stents and shunts are increasing lifespans, retinal prostheses and cochlear implants are enhancing impaired senses. And as technology improves, so the likelihood of using a prosthetic, orthotic, implantable or wearable during our lifetime increases.

I drive on. Whatever was blocking the road has cleared and I feel the vibration of the accelerator pedal through my prosthetic.

I'm at the frontier. I'm with the pioneers.

(From *Hybrid Humans*, Profile Books, 2022)

HOLD MY BREATH AS
I WISH FOR DEATH

Kathleen Nicholls

Thinking Outside the Box

There's a running joke between a few of my colleagues and I that I talk about death too much, to the extent that they holler and ring an imaginary bell at my first mention of death on any given day. It makes us laugh and boosts my reputation as a not-so-secret goth who defies convention by wearing hot pink. But mainly I like this silly routine because I am obsessed with death. I am obsessed with the complexities of living and then, one day, just not.

(FYI: This week I hit a new record of 08:02am when I mentioned craving "the cold earth of the grave" because I had upwards of 6 emails to deal with).

I'm not particularly morbid. (Although by this point you may already disagree with that). Often the mere mention of death physically repels people around me; they find it too uncomfortable and creepy to talk openly about the idea of dying.

Only it isn't an 'idea' it's a fact—an inevitability. The only one we all share.

My feelings on death have fluctuated wildly through the years. As a child I distinctly remember telling my very Catholic mother that I was terrified of the idea of 'eternal life'; I have to live for 80 years (maybe nearer 60; I am Scottish after all . . .) then start all over again?! NO THANK-YOU LORD! I'll pop downstairs if you don't mind.

As I got older, I spoke a lot about death with my grandmother, who was open about her own faith and excited to see her husband again in the afterlife. (Doesn't say much for my conversation to be fair but I'll let that one slide). I watched my beloved grandmother become ill and tired of life, and I watched her die. This was the first big loss in my life and I still to this day find it hard to think of her without welling up. I adored her and I miss her. Seeing her die disturbed me greatly and shook out of me the idea that death is always peaceful. It's not; it can ravage the body, cause great pain, and become something that is longed for despite an innate need to live.

When I became ill myself in my early twenties my view on death changed again. I quickly encountered the great challenge of 'staying alive' when every cell in your body wants to call it a day and pop down to the heated basement. The exhaustion in simply existing with a chronic illness can take an intense toll on the mind as well as the body and finding the enthusiasm for a life that can often feel consumed with misery is . . . difficult to say the least. So, I think about death and have thought about death for many years and continue to. I think about it when I feel low and how it would feel fine to just let go and go. I think about it when I feel good and panic that one day I'll have to go. I think about it when I feel joy and remember I have an illness that will likely shorten my time here. At times I panic at the thought of it and at times I relish the prospect.

I know how all of this must sound if you are reading this as someone without an incurable illness. I know because I've seen the horror on the faces of those who love and loathe me, at the mention of my relatively relaxed attitude to death. They think I'm depressed, or suicidal or have a literal death wish. I admit I've been all those things, but not now, and not in the eyes of those who I know and love who also suffer from a chronic condition. Some of these friends I've lost to illness, and as hard as that has been its also served to help me understand how fleeting it all is, and how important it is to LIVE while you are alive. How horrifying the end can be and how freeing. I've known those who have accepted it and those who never could.

Talking about death and indeed grief isn't something that happens commonly in the treatment and continued care of those with chronic illness. I suppose it doesn't need to be in the cases where it seems far off, and really why would you bring up something so distressing in the process of trying to get your patients 'better'? But for me, the lack of discussion around what is essentially an inevitability only serves to frighten me. Why is something that will happen sooner or later shrouded in such dark clothing? Why are we conversationally dressed like a funeral before the event? If we are to prepare ourselves for the full onslaught of what our illness may entail why shouldn't we know what may happen as our condition progresses to its final form?

I admit I may be in the minority in this but talking about death doesn't frighten me. Death itself does, sometimes. But it's out of my control, just like my illness. I can try my best to eat correctly, get enough rest, take my medication, and get my check-ups, but it doesn't stop my illness from absolutely flooring me when I least expect it. It's unpredictable and upsetting and like all toxic relationships, we dance through life together in a warped sort of co-dependent tango. I politely ask for it not to kill me, and it obliges, for now. But in accepting life ends and does indeed go on, I feel a strange sort of peace when my illness feels all-consuming.

I love my life and I am sad that part of that life involves a condition which causes me, and often those I love, distress. But I'm also fascinated with the beauty of living on in the minds and hearts of those who have loved me when I do have to go. If I leave before I'd have liked because that's what my genes have decided then so be it, but I'd like to be thought of kindly. Maybe people will remember me for my frankly show-stopping impression of the Bee Gees Barry Gibb circa 1998, or how great my jugs looked in a corset in early 2005, but I'd mainly like them to remember me for being kind, because it's all we have to offer one another. The kindness of nurses, doctors, strangers, and those around me have helped me cope with my condition in immeasurable ways, and as someone who has often had no option but to leave her life in the literal hands of others, kindness is a priceless currency.

Talk about death, don't talk about death; it's up to you. It's your one life and you can live it as you choose. But allow those of us who are perhaps more closely acquainted with it to occasionally discuss funeral plans over a fishbowl of Mojito without judgement. We will love you for it and may even include you in our will.

(FAO my colleagues: Time of death mention today: 12:48pm)

Dan O'Brien

From *Survivor's* Notebook

Past

Often we'd pass each other in our childless years, the two of us running our daily routes through the neighborhood. She was tiny, with a billowy veil of frizz. Did she notice me too? And why was she free in the middle of the day? Was she an artist like me? I worried she was anorexic or exercise-bulimic, at least. Saddled with a chauvinist for a husband or something worse. She was pregnant when my wife was. Later we'd pass each other frazzled, pushing our bawling strollers; if we paused to talk I feared we would kiss. Then my wife's diagnosis—there was no time to waste. They harvested her eggs the day after her surgery. I drove her at dawn from the hospital to the clinic and a doctor who appeared regularly on a reality TV show. My wife was sedated but still flinching, furiously cursing when I took a turn sharply, or hit a bump or a pothole. An oxygen tank clanked in the back seat (in case she had trouble with her breathing). My cramping was racking; I was only six months away from my own diagnosis. A pretty, yawning young nurse ushered me into a brightly lit closet with a wipeable recliner and a flat-screen TV (cycling through a soft-focused slideshow of fountains and flowers) and told me to "use the plastic cup." Six or seven eggs were fertilized but nothing took. Then I was wiped clean too. During my chemotherapy I'd sometimes shamble past that neighborhood woman with her new baby, the first one toddling. And just this arsenic hour as I trudge along in my remission, my pending cure, I behold: she has begotten a third. One marches, one skips, one tosses a teething toy over the lip of the well-used stroller. We pass on the sidewalk outside a watering hole that's roaring like a rapids.

New Hampshire

Pursued by a blue pit bull leashed to a girl in floral rain boots crying no Midnight no

Ativan

Now a pill; but in the hospital a needle's kiss: dispersion, then a notion of milk leaking through blinds as my mind crept from bed toward my only sensible desire

Use

We used to clean ourselves. Then we hired two women who claimed to be sisters, though one was loquacious and flirtatious while the other sister wasn't. From a country where as children they witnessed beheadings fully funded by our parents' taxes. They left us soon after my wife's surgery—all the pill bottles and stained bandages in the trash and we understood: they hadn't signed on for this. We found another cleaner when I got sick. She was quiet, and she worked so thoroughly that our things could be hard to find. She'd restore our pill bottle caps to our pill bottles, ordering and stacking them away as if we no longer needed them. Which funnily enough has me thinking of the urologist with the urine-colored hair, who reminded me testily of my late stage, after I'd insisted on twilight sedation before I would permit him to poke around inside my bladder to extract the necrosis and sew me up properly this time. My wife stormed out, a rogue wave. The urologist would rather be surfing, and had other patients besides. An older nurse confided that her daughter, born coincidentally the same year as me, she said, had cancer, a rare form in her case and

"Look she's still alive!" This was when I broke down, something I'd never done with a stranger before, and she rocked me shushing from side to side. We clean house ourselves now. Again. Thanks to them (and so many others) I sit here at my desk, working, such as it is, trying in my mostly self-serving way to be of use.

Ativan 2

Recuperating from surgery when I couldn't stand to sleep, and before the chemotherapy, when dying was impossibly likely, I had to find a way out of the house. But the catheter (my stitched-up bladder was leaking) scraped my insides like a melon baller with every wincing step toward the gleaming operating table of the Pacific at high noon. Everybody was doing whatever they could. While I yearned to cry aloud: I am crushed beneath a storm-toppled tree. My house has fallen in upon me. As I waited for the drug to douse my brain. Already I was tolerating; I knew I'd receive only a blossoming reprieve in which my fists uncurled. A window through which I could see myself walking.

Sprain Road

Early evenings in winter we'd see an old woman walking determinedly from one end of town to the other and back again a figure of reliable ridicule to us children how she whipped her hips elbows wrists around bustling probably compulsively oftentimes in rain sleet snow navigating icy sludge salt floes plowed mounds and now I know she was a survivor like me exorcising her anxiety along the red and white striating byways believing strenuous repetition might keep her future flowing cleanly believing as I do there is safety in witnessing though I do not recall her carrying a light

Ativan 3

Because I am alive almost a year after treatment the doctor prescribes a therapeutic tapering. I praise and snap the white tablet in half. The sun is leached of light; metallic. As ever. The fountain in the courtyard runs dry: bed of stones, no change. Paranoia refloods the brain. I am certain they despise and defame me. If they remember me. I abhor the tenacity of my dear demons. Is this who I am truly? I concede I am losing it yet I demand to be heard. It doesn't matter. It's up to me to talk myself down. Get used to this (again).

Afterword

Maybe I'm wrong: it goes on. We inherit, we rent. Our song is made melodic with pain. Upset, cascading. Respiring, ablaze. Winter's rain rinses the slight air. My daughter's hair grows while fig trees possess eternity. We illuminate each other: The hummingbird eats the spider. Coyotes digest the genius of crows. Animals are animals. And so on. "And the spaceship swallows the whale?" She thinks this is the end. Yes, I surprise her, as we fly away to another planet.

William Erickson

Two Poems

The Deaths That There Are

On Tuesday there is fog
but on Wednesday, no fog.
In the last mile of sky
before space i thought
the ghosts of the recently
dead would collect, as if
against glass beyond
which the air is all
the ghost there can be.
But what's true is only
that either there's fog
or there's not, and
the very recently dead
are exactly like fog,
how it lifts and descends,
how its beads on the leaves
are too heavy sometimes
for the trees to hold up.
This thing in your fingers
is all yours to touch.
There's a way and
the way is a death but the death
is this bloom on the stem.

Baby Teeth

i sit outside in the weather
and listen for languages.
Not just people's
languages but languages that
aren't languages.
Languages that reach
like sped-up tree roots inside,
how they follow what
feeds them until they
exhaust it and how when
they do it's so quiet
like the quiet of the baby
i still somehow contain.
We speak and
we speak and
we speak and
i don't even
think we know
what words mean.

Mark DuCharme

"Your Message Here" & Other Poems

Two Poems: A Bestiary

I. Birds

Forget actionable sin items

Repeat the sweat of
Angels at bowling tournaments

It's useless to be who you
Already are

Leave behind
Your login, in dark humming

Think like birds
Whose friends undo you

II. Whales

I'm lazy but I'm working all the time
Sky isn't a mispronunciation of fate

Is your wallet an amulet?
Can you breathe the devices of those who pass by

With nothing to say again anyway
Except in bungalows or still-birthed catalogues?

The rain where I went is left yesterday
If you're foregrounded, don't forget to twitch

In sodden beast examples
Whether or not the whales continue to despise us

A Fable, for García Lorca

I don't want to listen
Until we think like animals

The child knows more about evil

He is here tonight

He comes bearing rotten fruit
Or dead birds' eyes

It is an image of an image
That fills up
The blank night sky—

The sky cannot possibly be
Other than itself

I went looking for you, when you were still not here
I went looking for dead, insufficient tomorrows

In a fable of your voice, & all it
Soothes—

Crying out in dullness
For lost children, who hunt stones

As precious, sacred artifacts
That the hungry earth entombs

In deadpan humor, & our gross
Complicity—

Wake not the fidgety
Only to bleed them

The past is also a distraction

A division, or a way
Of feeding
On those who bore us (who bear this earth)

Like you who hardly ever weave
Amid the incitements of stillborn eyes

When we wake, against some furtive

Hungry moon—

Dr. Mabuse, L'Écrivain

Surveillance at the videographer's
Failed in the most innovative ways

It's no use going back
The doctor is no longer where you see him

Even if we gathered, took up space
Put roots down

In frantic speech, the hindered
Will not soon believe

In their know-it-all foretelling
In deleted content streams

That shrill romance is through
As the man in the hat writes in crayon dust

The empire of mocking is sick of your thrill
Let me put it to you as only an explosives expert might

Let me swallow the wind with chalk crayon eyes
The great counterfeiters are no more among us

Lonesome in gnarled orchards
Where menacing villagers twist & turn in grief

Your Message Here

What price shiny
In broken rejoinders
Rustling our tongues?

I await the bare minimum
Eking out a compendium
Of awkward silence held ajar

In the fault lines of our tenderness
In commodities of understanding
I is not other than you is a syllogism

A photomosaic of contingent fault lines
Look not on paper when the shooting starts
Gather flora for a lark in your arms

Become impacted by songbirds
In the air about you no one grieves
The things that must go on

I leave them here for further study
We are there & what we are
When we are all astray

Exulting in tarmacs for my relief
Where, late, I'll find us there
Like a reverse story problem or a set of crystals

In the end, you said you would not go
That tears may flow like prizes
In the air about no one names

The things that must go on
I leave them here for your review
Name the animal who most fears you

Tenderly, upon redaction
While the heat blurs & is swept aside
In sensitive, grieving verse

Which diminishes the common
While the red earth cleaves
& I reassure myself that I am bony

A credit to my industry
However much the lakes have now unraveled
Tight words on a shallow page

The one who posted in the chat
Saying "great last line" clearly had
Misheard it

Heat brims with autumn's eyes
Poetry is a syllogism
Distracted by your eyes

I hang out in the language & spell
Out my misgivings
In a flicker of upheaval

When silence heals all broken sparrows
You skim
I dabble

The word a loaded room
Birth attached to brick but amplified
I lapse in fatal voiceovers

I'll linger in your ancient book & wither
I'll design a city
Where birth is full as death

The poem I don't want
Is there, its edges
Throbbing

Incited on your watch while I
Stay up
In cul-de-sacs lacking theory

Paper urchins, null surprise
The thought tank was a truck heap
I picture you there

Far from any light source
But with the freedom
To die young

I knew where I was when I said I was lost
Sometimes, I couldn't leave
With ridiculous set pieces, in my idiom

Let me know the terror where I dwell
Undo the winter of your worst sleepover
I used to be then, but now I'm gone

There is peace
In the valley, I believe
& Ideas move like ancient trains

Lines' meanings change
By degrees
Whether or not it lies upon the tongue

In fault lines of a tenderness
Rustled tongues
Rare mirth an obverse scrawl

Cal Freeman

"Echo's" & Other Poems

Echo's

The quality of the perch isn't why
a restaurant succeeds or fails, but I miss
the pan-fried perch they had at Echo's. Fresh Lake Erie perch,
lightly-breaded, a recipe the family would never divulge
when I asked them. I never caught their names,
but I feel awful they didn't make it.
When I was a kid, this place
was called Chaim Sweeney's and
Charlie Taylor used to sing here (there?),
and unless you heard him do
"The Wild Colonial Boy" and "The Flower
of Sweet Strabane," you likely have no affinity
for this place. Affixing new names
to buildings without structurally changing them
does a lot for ambiance though.
It gives an architecture to memories real
and imagined, personal or channeled
from the muddled anachrony of décor,
the palimpsestic layering of linoleum and wallpaper.
Chaim Sweeney was the world's foremost authority
on the hamburger, the menu said,
and I wouldn't blame anyone for thinking
this was bombast since the hamburgers
at the eponymous restaurant were unremarkable.
I'd ride in the backseat of my grandmother's Ford Escort wagon
down Outer Drive, that high curving road
commissioned by the WPA
to ribbon the perimeter of Detroit,
that uncompleted road, that floodplain
tracing the southern bend of the cantankerous Ecorse River,
to hear old Charlie sing. He'd let me sit at the edge
of the stage and strum Irish rebel songs
on my plastic guitar during his breaks.
Chaim Sweeney pissed his money
out the door on live entertainment,
which is ostensibly an enticement
to draw beer drinkers in,
but Echo's was doomed at the naming.
I think of Echo's story and a

caterwaul of the gone rings out
drowns the preening boy
and lifts him off in the face of half-voiced
predation
he was not so special they never are

she chattered nonsensically during Jove's trysts
to slow Juno's pursuit who deleted
all prefixes muted vocatives
the effect only approximating the sound
of sound returning she clutched
the leaning putrefaction
the boy in putrefaction in tableau
as what she once was ossified
and was chiseled into a practice chanter
for oblivion what could be more loved
than what was almost lived in
gone marmoreal memorial *I'm yours*
and all the business *enjoy my body*
and all the unpleasant business
of malediction parroted with a banality
charming as charmed Ah me
to repeat *Ah me*
as the business goes belly-up

I wanted to talk about the songs
of a dead folk singer who was friends
with my grandparents, a man who could
describe your sad sack story back to yourself
like Demodocus at the Mead Hall on Scherie.
I wanted to talk about perch and the imperiled
fisheries of Southeast Michigan, the restaurants
where the fishers sent their catches.
The phosphorous in the fields, the lyngbya in the harbor.
The reference to Lake Erie
I found while reading *Finnegan's Wake*
in Echo's Restaurant one January afternoon—
our lake lemanted, that greyt lack . . .
urban and orbal, though seep froms umber
under wasseres of Erie. The owner asked,
"Did it stop for a merciful moment, the ice storm?"
It had me thinking of the adjective "merciful" because I'm also scared
all the time of death and money,
of paucity and grift, by what might arrive in the mail
with the clap of tin, by excessive bilirubin
in the blood (can't be a liver and have a liver,
the ale taster in the night-book says).
I'd watch the Lions at Echo's every Sunday
while reading a book and eating perch,
which sounds a lot like losing in Loserville
but the Lions have a way of getting you to pay
attention, which is to say they have unique
ways of losing, ways you haven't yet imagined.
They slow the awful sabbath down.
There's rarely such a chance to gaze languorously
inward and taste the afternoon like a morsel
(egg, flour, lemon, tartar sauce, the flesh of freshwater).

Note-Taking While Listening to "Floyd, the Barber"

The barber is bored. On nights like this, he's not a barber. His hair gets unruly. It might be wise for him to quell the barber's boredom and bad luck by sitting himself in one of his own chairs and praying for a hand to appear.

He doesn't think the rats are an individual rat when he sees one run through his yard on consecutive nights. What runs once is what others attend to while thinking of springing into action. Credulous people believe a single act proliferates but not that others are prolific. A barber knows differently in sweeping hair from linoleum.

The heart is as much of an implement as a pair of scissors. There are things to say about spirits, hearts, and bodies, and sometimes the three are synonyms. Sometimes the ogival moonlight pierces him like a scissor and makes for a long subsequent day.

He counts hairs strewn across the floor of his memory. The actuary can't count on longevity any more than the barber can. It's funny that the appellation "the barber" is correctly preceded by a comma in the song title, but it makes sense. Pointless punctiliousness is the quintessence of barbering.

It's Labor Day, after dark, and the people south of Dartmouth are confused, or they've failed to calibrate the recursive nature of the recent past to the recent present. He's walking through somebody else's trash night and remembering what matters most. Not the flattening of a Low E a whole step to D; he wouldn't think of it, just as many of us refuse to think of the constituent parts that make us.

A silver maple leaf soughs in the lawn. A stain glass lamp shade mutes the incandescent light in a living room. The most impressive barrel is the one with the address spray-painted in silver on the side. They don't know (the ignominious they with their doorbell cameras and fictive renderings of the multifarious threats afflicting us) that the holiday will set their pick-up back.
Day, holiday, he knows nothing of their pasts.

He, himself, here comes everyone, contemplating what scurries around the corner in ground cover (myrtle is indelibly like hair) at the sides of buildings, what scurries into the open (he saw a Cooper's Hawk the other day on a fence down by the creek) at its own peril, believes that contingencies necessitate calendars and existences like this one are full of contingent plans.

No tone or cowlick is special. A widow maker rubbing against a neighbor tree sounds exactly like a chair cranking up to a barber's height. A taxidermized deer above a mirror is no better than a plastic one. "There used to be more to work with up here," he tells me as he stares into the sky, as I crumple into the chair.

A Grove

Everything runs away
in a hazy instant (everyone).
The sleet is in the iris,
past the price of succulents
and nursers instransitive
as Haworth sterning shame
among pate-dry meadows.
There's no mnemonic,
no box of salvaged picket
as we bank against a deluge
of improbables, yet
that which begins in kitsch
often culminates in floodlit
violence. Non-sequiturs,
birds among the bramble
lifting off,
the sun behind a blear
of diesel fumes like a candle
in a half-roundel.

Papilio Machaon

The swallowtail is a perennial instar
in its own story, a metamorphosis, an imago

in the unbearable house of light, just as each
person is a disguise against a range of predations

dreamed up in the vague apologue of the mind.
Here are a few devices to ward them off—

cream-colored slashes on the edges of black crepe;
an everted repugnatorial osmeterium

splayed like a yellow Y or a snake's tongue;
the emission of aliphatic acids and sesquiterpenes;

a shield carried on the darkling road through Troy
and a gap-toothed scowl (Machaon, heroic eponym);

a quarter rest, a caesura in a staff of dirt;
a tumble like a knuckleball through heavy air.

*

Your poor mother, somebody says.
Not even equipped with a guidebook

to tell her what you are,
while in the chairlift of her dotage,

she offers exculpatory colloquialisms
for wayward boys

slurred with a tongue slowed
and swollen by shot nerves.

She watches from her bay window
because she knows one day something

that overwinters will survive
in its hibernaculum of leaf-sewn twig

and emerge profligate, windswept
as the horizon cast in scrims of rain.

Sorry Saturday Was Like Money

I tried to rent a cottage for a week,
but they were all taken.
My mother thinks
I've already escaped
in mind what geography
has staked me to.
Vague generalities accumulate
like interest. This paucity
of verbs. A possum.
Several chimney swifts.
You should see me smile.
It's strained for the teeth
crook out the womb
or in the maw of God
who for all we know
is not only crooked, but happy.

Elizabeth Robinson

Three Poems

Proverb

Cold fingers twined
through
warm fingers measure
relative
life, when measurement
is
relative intimacy.

Word Problem

A hand held to a mirror cannot see itself. A hand held up, high enough, drains fingers of blood, absorbs mercury, holds the image of hand to the image of hand: one cold, one warm.

The hand reaches through relative darkness to find its partner. Not left to right, but right to left. A dimly remembered joke that asks, "What's left?" Remainder of light makes reflection, and so the problem completes itself. A measurement that forgets to question, a solution rinsed away as circulation ceases in the uplifted hand.

The Plural of "Math" is "Maths"

The interviewer asks "Have you always?" And the answer is yes, always. As a hand clings to a hand. Always the brevity of the hand. Always the spaces between.

The way a hand on a child refuses to learn. The way the child's insistence on touch supercedes knowing. Place the hand on a stove to imprint the red coil. Lift the red ember as though it will turn liquid on contact with skin.

Brevity is a symptom of the aggregate. The thumb added to the index to the middle finger to the ring finger to the pinkie.

Brevity is a symptom of the aggregate as a hand is a mirror of a hand. Count this. The fingertips poised. The touch of the counterpart.

A hand stroking the hand of a dying woman. Almost too firmly.

Memory is another method of addition. The index finger tracing the outline of the opposing hand, finger by finger. An eros that makes the mouth open. A way to break breath, also, into discrete segments.

The parts imply control. Or offer the fragment as its own emotion. Whoever portrays a single finger? We are always ready to imagine *fingers. Hand. Hands.*

The hand grasped and pulled forward is not a complete equation.

The empty-handed. Even that is additive.

Always the nursery rhyme, the counting game, the chant that puts story on top of number.

Carpals. Metacarpals. Phalanges. Remember the plastic model that could be disaggregated in sections. Bones sheeny and unbreakable.

Five. Ten.

Fifteen. Larger than itself. Twenty. Fingers placed, as though casually, between fingers. Count this. A caloric. A temperature. Where warmth conjoins, a final product, over the boundaries of pulse.

Jack Foley

The Onlie Critic

have you noticed
that all the critics
of Wallace Stevens'
"The Only Emperor
is the Emperor
of Ice Cream"
have trouble fitting in
some of the details
of the poem?
Helen Vendler
accounts for the curds
by saying that there is food
at funerals, especially at
funerals that occur
in places Stevens
occasionally visited.
I don't believe she explains
why the curds should be
concupiscent.
has a single critic
who has written about the poem
suggested that the two stanzas
of the poem
take place in different places?
what are those big phallic cigars—
usually distributed after a birth—
doing at a funeral?
what exactly might
concupiscent curds
and kitchen cups
refer to?
to whom are the boys bringing
flowers?
none of these things
are in the second stanza.
I think the reason is that
there is no funeral
in the first stanza
and no sexuality
in the second.
they take place
in different worlds,
the world of life
and lust
in the first stanza
and the world of death
and poverty
in the second,
though both these worlds
lead to the same
sad assertion:
alas
that ice-cream
should melt.
the only critic
is the critic
of water as it flows.

Tom La Farge

From *Insomnia Jazz*

Spreadingly, blurringly

Opera where there should have been jazz. Opera. It pushes you. Draws a line, you on one side and on the other . . . opera. How can you believe in it?

It makes you ask, also, how can you believe in you? It's in Italian, and in Orchestra–and you? You have some contrary assertion? Can you hammer, can you push, can you even go to sleep? Cross the line between waking and sleep, but if you can't, then permit some inverse absorption, ink into porous paper, and accept the opera. You could be the sleep. Let the dream now write itself spreadingly, blurringly on your resistant treacherous surface. If you could drink in temperate and equal draughts, would it be opera, would it be jazz? Insomnia has to be good for something: a looseness of grip on the pen, a certain illegibility. It's the sleep-in-waiting, the incomplete surrender. In collapse no surprise but in the agony of balance, the unsatisfaction of waver, not knowing what to drink to precipitate oblivion or attention.

Foraging down lanes not clearly mapped, not off the map, headed for the battlefield, but in which war? Wisdom silent. Opera fills the air.

Go don't try

Food when the weather's too hot. Love when you're stymied. Nothing new coming over the radio. Bad air, bad art. Make a taste, but nothing to combine but a day's worth of mouthwash. Stories hiding behind grudges. Words: they were all fastened to the wrong notes. Nothing came to life. Nothing so solid on Broadway as hot cotton air. We are sweating ghosts in wrong clothes, disappearance preventers.

Go don't try. Travel instead of being the train. They tore the tracks up today, tomorrow they open fire. Then stop missing them. They won't miss you, the angels.

You know it's around somewhere. Just caught on something. Something dull and jagged. Make it move. Cook it till it marries. Respell it. Nobody's waiting for you.

Energetically dead

(a duet)

Voice imports direction like a charm.

Speak loud, speak volumes!

Exposition is an imposition.

A posture of imposture!

A fear of impending expense?

Impressive expressions!

Imperial experience.

It's the extra version.

Complicated implication!

Don't refuse confusion.

Who's extending intending?

Who's concluding excluding?
Introduce me to your seducer.
Produce your greengrocer.
Refine his mortal grossness.
Confine your defining, in fine.

Mind your matter!
All I ask
is tools to dig
myself out.

Sounds grave.

My life is not to be borne.

Still unborn?

Energetically dead.

Hard at it.
It's a crooked style–
don't be cross.

Waterlogged,
settling in
a spiral.

Leak before you loop.

Take your way to weather

(duet)

Answer my need to dust.

Take your way to weather.
Or know.

Once new no longer safe.
Needs weigh, whether I owe
upheaval in an air
of induced gravity. How
much longer can I
bear up? I hate to wait.

O folly clear the woe
for a little lighter load
the road rounds the turn
past the passage way
up ahead.

Weigh my head and see
what you figure it at!
I'm tired. Can't you spell me?

I'll take your watch
when it's worth my time
in the meantime keep
your hands to yourself.

Don't come back for seconds.

I've been taking your whine
for hours

Why not? Compress me!

but now it's time
to drift your catch
course your plot
weigh your pick
line the undertow
level the keep

I don't get you, can you be
a little more contiguous to me?

I'm the line of least resistance
I'm the reigning circumstance.

I didn't bring my umbrella.

You're already all wet
whether or no

I know.

That's a relief.

That's a notion that should
tide me over.

See, now you knew.

There are lush musics that surge and move me into my bed
big beyond voice
taking musics
unblind, willful, catching up lesser histories
driving over duties into delight in going
and it's too bad that musics of this kind must
advance in just the one time
or I could wash up here
or there.

Enlarging loss.
I am not a tossed body.
It is not a storm of dance.
I am a sail proceeding into hollow of air
shielded from musics by me.

Not every horn is a trumpet
spiral of brightness
not always a going there
winding in on
or flinging away from
yearning in bright dark space
call to a somber flutter or sober tap
ground to figure
hiss in answer to wail over throbbing.

You can write words to music
because there are no words in music
but there is light and yearning
for what light might play on.

Jail to Motor

(a duet)

Jail to motor, violation

turns battery to drive

into a night not known

for frozen light not

to be put out

shut down.

Armor postures

Love played its part in keeping

local love, jammed

listening

Just a thought gone to fragments

mineral tinklings against

impenetrable hull

exploded residue of

of long-ago events

musical now for
the dropping-out of
most of the matter

shattered into a history
arriving periodically

flutter

sliding tone
static packing
the sense of
"out there"

R.S. Mengert

Three Poems

The Price

I wear my stomach on the outside
to spite the sea.

It wasn't always thus.
Once, I was content

to keep my stomach stashed
in the abdominal cavity, so I could pass

with all the well-heeled kids
at that expensive school across the tracks

where I was bussed. These were people
who could eat

whenever they wished. Their pasts
were easy, futures bright.

And with my stomach on the inside, I
could pass. The sea

would let me pass. Then, the sea left me
alone, staring at the endless beige

beyond as all the vast sea shrank
far into the retreating horizon. After that

I could no longer front.
Years. Decades. I could not guess how long

I've worn my stomach on the outside
now. If I can do it of necessity, I can do it

out of spite. My back hurts
from carrying my guts.

I cannot lie down to sleep.
I have not sat down

to dinner at the table in some years.
Dry, and cracked, the leather sack

around me will not leave me
in peace. But that's the price of spite.

So fuck the sea, fuck the stomach,
fuck the body

fuck food.
I never could swim anyway.

Vision of the Present

In the eternal night of memory, it is quiet now.
The lighthouse burns
before the ship sees land.
My hometown lies at the bottom of the lake.
Tears evaporate in the dark. Inside
every deposed god of daylight
is a watch with a cracked lens.
Time is gridlock: black lines, white squares.
Stairs and ledges, faces
forming in the perfect dark.
Mistakes so big
they might as well be murder.
Fires lit by books and photos.
This is the last time you will see me alive.
These affairs
always worked out in the past
if we only said the right things.

Post Human Condition

"I am not an author. I think authors are assholes."
—Michael Burkard

If an author were writing this, it would take place in New York. One of those neon urban nightspots—sparse, white, black, and grey, pipes exposed, drainpipes for table legs, all the sentimental markers of decay. The spot itself would not be named. That would be too obvious. The only thing obvious would be that the story takes place in New York, so you would know that I, the author, live, or lived (if only for a six-week internship) in New York. New York City. Not upstate. Not New Jersey. Maybe Brooklyn. Not the Bronx.

Maybe I (the protagonist is always an "I," though we are not to think for one moment that it is autobiographical) would be snorting coke like the "you" in some slick neon magenta novel from about 30 years prior. Coke designates the loneliness and alienation of the "I" staring into the void (the "I" is very sensitive and profound). Once, "I" might have been shooting smack, but not now. Smack is trashy. Smack is for people who live in trailers and have never been to New York. Smack is for New Jersey. Authors don't use smack. "I" am an author (though this is not autobiographical), and "I" snort coke. In New York. Never smack.

Meanwhile, outside, in New York (did I mention this was in New York?), let's just say Manhattan since Brooklyn is just as out of reach now, outside in the mean New York City streets of Manhattan, the glass and concrete towers crumble, the Hudson boils, phosgene gas seeps into the air from beneath the sewer grates and manholes and cracks in the sidewalk, hedge fund bankers flay vagrants alive and wear their skins for protection, stars turn to lava and melt out of the sky and scorch the ground below, and "I" (not "you") snort coke (not smack or crank, that's trashy), and look at all the neon and the pipes and the coke and the 40 dollar drinks and the beautiful hollow women and the beautiful hollow men and lament my sorry ass for coming from Nebraska and knowing I must move soon to New Jersey, because I, you must see, am an author in New York.

Three Poems

A Kindred Spirit: Unidentified B&W Photo of Woman with Bat

The woman with the bat perched
wings outstretched on her head
stares ahead fixed like the bat's
a book she must keep still to keep

level. Life in the back then black
and white possessed intense tint.
Photo tucked within all those letters
bundled with a brittle rubber band

stuffed into a moldy manila envelope
marked, "from the first three months
of college," all those letters from
daughter to mother signed, "All My Love,"

"With Dearest Love to you," "With
Much, Much Love, Your Own,"
"Love Always," "All Love from Your
Daughter," "Dearest One," "Darling."

Where does all my love go?
As if there's a deep top hat
perched atop a head to catch
all lighter-than-air love, maybe

love's a rabbit pulled from that
bottomless well by its ever-
loving ears, and before our eyes
—POOF—it's a bird, but not

a dove, something blacker
with its mesh wings outspread
to dry from all that cascading
love dripping from its body,

sun to do its bright evaporation.
Could we live off love's photo-
synthesis? I can't help but wonder
if there was more love back

in those black & white days,
more love sung straight from
hearts less burdened by irony,
sarcasm, the hard laugh that

comes with nihilism, or the
I-Told-You-So smirk. No I know
no one today who would dress
funeral best and plop a bat

atop her head. That kind of love
is dead. Long live love. Bats only
live twenty years or so. That
doesn't seem long enough.

Hands vs. Ears

Some say a little fiction in the ear
is better than a fact in the hand.
Touch, a blunt instrument and blind,
where the ear folds sound like cold dough
layered into golden flakes of fabric,
an oven of enhancement, a seashell
of oceanic dimensions. I shouldn't be
so hard on hands, I know, but fingers
always grasp at facts, want to feel
proportions and set hooks in
like surveyor's stakes, some kind of
ownership in touch I blanche at.
The ear lets all pass through its
finest sieves, drum without skin, dream
catcher of wind. I side with the holes
on the sides of the head. They can
keep their ten digits and fill them
with their hold on air. I will go diving
into that blue, blue water I can still hear.

War is a time to flee, so I gave in to my desire
to be as disappointing as possible. Seized

by this song, I took a hallway headed for the stars
but I saw an earth baby at my feet barking, *don't*

leave me here, mama. If you are my son, you've done
a very good job disguising yourself. But still how could

I do anything but discontinue. You took me by surprise.

My poems about babies always disappoint me
because their tragedies echo mine. I feel the need

for a good base line, something I can dance to. Let's go
back to Ohio, if it's still there. When we arrive, you'll see
my legs hanging in the high school trophy case. Don't worry,
my boy, we can use them as wings to finally get us some air.

Greg Bem

Figures

1: Musing

The crack is the rupture inside. The lines form crooked to the horizontal. Dreams are beautiful and chaotic. The hands are enflamed and jagged. Winged fingers. Ruptured bubbles within microscopic crevasse. Moonlit airplane sinking across to escape. And the wizards wait. And the witches choke on cackle. On highway alert, rumble of fiction. Imagine just out of sight of the interstate.

Imagine that and I am coughing through peace. Diadem of karmic gesture. The completed jester's smile. Home again, a safety net, a safer Net, an etiquette to bind them, and in their hearts the binding is glowing and growing. It can't be stopped. It can't be. We will be consumed, dwarfed by replay, the result, the reverb. We will be consumed, con, a con, the Mac Low Eon instance.

Just in time: justice, in time as I write this, right this.

2: Them

The Drone Woman

Less about the human than the carriage. Carrying age, carrying life of our age.
This is the speech with which we birth, circuit blood and broken spines, slippage.
And the meander through a pit-scape of ohs and ones, what's it even say?
What's even it mean? Hallmark of the creators, the robot pleasantly demonic,
blue eyes gazing into my abyss, of limited possibility, and we're all attached to hip,
we're all diming our way through time's latest, the "say" of sooth and the errs of our ways.

The Ghost Knight

Herald of mist and slew, slough and what's missed, what's been missing, really,
what have we been dreading with the lengthening of days, more of an exposure, really,
the lines getting longer, the lies playing out louder, liars challenging sour,
and I am a pondering being, slipping in and out of the purvey, the periphery,
the puff puff bliss of history, and the wash is a light, cloudy blue, cloudy eyes,
mistakenly foggy, but the devil is in the details, where we get lost and stand, violently, still.

The Radioactive Man

At the poet's keep, a book with a cover with two beings lacking faces,
south lake where we go to find the canny connections, a canopy for hummingbirds
and cobwebs, a place lightly lit by a mooted sun, muted, mutant, mutate,
and the ochre suit matches the ochreish face, also blank, I spun it around, I hid it,
I'm ogrish, malevolent benefactor, the sinners in my hands, my anger disruptive.
The thin, black gun represents vacuums and the vacuous, pushing and pulling at once.

The Samurai

It is the katana that forms, thin slice of whole, slice of thought, sliced, rotted, at once.
An earlier memory where I'm passing aisles of filthy books, thinking perhaps I'm rotten.
And perhaps it's a ronin, masterless, dead masters on thinly sliced floors, clean,
corners and ridges, etches, meaty palaces, thin slip of rounded beam, wood like bone,
    bracing heavens,
passage towards made by body's breath, an elegance unlike the Maoist quote on a Samurai
    website,
where have I gotten, found myself, in this lossless space, wilderness, kempt and upkept.

The Recidivist

Inching forward into the depths, memory comes to light after 12 years of entombment:
the Waldrops, loving Gizzi, loved the New Depths of Deadpan, and how could you not!
Knotted in the world, Ezmeralda and Bogota one moment, Aleksi Perälä and Lahti the next,
I dream in poetry that knots, that colludes, that jumps out of windows and tails it highly to
    the weeds,
never greasy, always chaffed, long dry spell sting of skin rubbing skin, blades upon blades,
figure rejoined, saga etc, continuity, bearish committal, suddenly I remember how resin can
    stick.

Madly a Scientist

Flock of dread spikes, the dreaded spike in the fluted chamber, greenly and wizened,
sickly you've become wise in your old brews, methods of Bunsen decades long in the make,
the way you wear your grin is a calm psychopathy, hiccup, run away with ye, goes the zone,
a kind of eureka blast toward Eureka hills, smell of weed-encrusted decision-making spills
across intersections, sinks in sticky to the heel, the world melting into Dalisean clockwork.
Meanwhile, lest we forget: a black glove, the green splatters, buttoned buttons, and the red
lenses.

Bowl in one hand, plastic in one hand, lift up, pour corn past teeth to mouth, and the chewing, and the swallowing into a throat's greeting. The eyes glaze over. What's missing? The nose crinkles. What's missing? The ears dry out and flake. What's missing? The neck grows bumps and loosens. What's—missing? Safe passage. Safe construction. Safer discussions. Safety has its place. You are in good hands. you are in, good hands. You are, in good hands.

On my way here there was a feather. And there was a myth. And the spilling of the beans. And the rickety footsteps along the rotted floorboards. And the night that spoke in corners and the boundaries of the lamplit curbs. Chirps from dead smoke detectors. A laundry list of constraints. Everything around a tool and a curse. Those wizards, those witches, that jester, that gesture. All comes crumbling down, into a puddle of something vaguely edible and objectively terrifying to the onlooker.

What's missing, what's missing. A smooth transition as the six have gone home to be with their masses and prayers.

WILL STANIER

On Our Way

Contrails tracing typos—
piercing clouds, needles
and thread.

On our way
horses look funny, bug-eyed, their
fly masks on.

There's a man with a dog tucked under
his arm, stopped on his bike chatting with a car.

A woman on our left-hand side
pushing a grocery cart, box of beer underneath,
another dog sitting up in the basket.

And so
thinking it over,
in spitting distance of love
(while also holding it here)

Every parking lot either empty or full
Sounds of traffic, susurrus of traffic.

I will talk too much
I will talk
I will write in my journal
only one thing:

Look! Clouds blowing fast.

Malcolm McCollum

Three Poems

One Pitcher's Story

—for Wade Arnold

I was throwing my usual—
fastball, slider, fastball,
change—but as I threw
the slider, my left hip went out,
Jiménez hopelessly dove
after the ball spinning behind him
through the cloud of dirt,
and I landed wrong
on my landing leg
and ripped up the middle,
and I couldn't pitch any more
for two years.

When I got back
I was always thinking,
"It could happen again,"
and I knew twice
would be one too many.
I never tried to throw
my best pitch
ever.
again.

So I went to coaching.
Watching the young ones close
to try to help them
do it right and not hurt themselves.

When I took my missus
to see the Eiffel Tower one time,
I saw all those pieces of steel
fanning up from the base,

looked like they were cheering
that little tower way up in the sky.
Next morning, shaving, looked at me,
nobody, looked. Said, "Okay."

Mourning Dove

A softly mourning dove
materialized to drink from the fountain
on the terrace where I worked,
resetting root-heaved flagstones.

I stopped, stooped, my head raised
to watch her drink and hear
the water splash itself.
I must have moved or made a sound,

and she was airborne, wheeling,
gone, only the sound her wings
made left behind. The sound
a playing card made in the spokes

of the black and red Schwinn
my Dad bought me. You fixed the card
to the back fender strut with wire,
bent it in, and off you went,

making a rising whirr, almost as if
you had a motorbike beneath you.
I went back to my work, wondering
where my time had gotten to.

The Last Vacant Lot in America

For nine years I've taken myself and my
dogs,
now old, to the last vacant lot in America,
a half acre left alone, officially a grade
school
playground. For me, a sacred place,
a field where nothing useful grows but grass
and weeds and a small grove of random
trees
down in the corner above the creek,
brindle green and tan and khaki
as the rains come and go and come again,
but down in the grove, even in winter,
some spruce show green to blue.

Last night a fox slipped under the fence
along the creek bank and smoked
through the high grass. My dogs
are so old they didn't even notice her.

Tonight the engines of improvement had arrived.
They'd ripped off half the field's scalp;
Roots lay in the rowelled dirt like severed fingers.
They'd dozered back the edges of the grove
and left the shreds of the improved trees
stacked like hay mows in the field.

A new steel fence kept the surviving trees back.
The old steel fence along the street,
erected to keep cars apart from children and dogs,
had been extracted, as if its roots might contain gold.

The engines had been busy. Now they rested,
huge, unbestial shapes in primary
yellow, red and blue, named for beasts
progress despises: caterpillar, deer, rhino.
They stood on the shadowed field
triumphant, madly sane and perfect,
as if M.C. Escher had come to visit.

A billboard in the school's front yard
and a line of young maples, planted as harbingers,
had proclaimed the advent of this progress.
All the maples had died of neglect since the board
went up. Architects' trees don't need care.

Sometimes the dogs and I would arrive
to find the whole field alive in crows,
bouncing and pecking and glowing black
in the dusk, and the dogs would leap
from the car and scatter them, scrawing,
into the oncoming night. Then the dogs
would come running back to me proud and slobbering.

The crows will still come,
and the foxes may, and geese will fly
over the playground perfect as the picture,
in which no children play.

P.J. Blumenthal

Where am I?

I live in the city of D. It's really a wonderful town, and soon we shall be celebrating the thousand year anniversary of its founding. I am particularly excited about this because I am on the planning committee for the celebrations which will last for two weeks and culminate in a grand spectacle on the exact date of the earliest historical reference to D. The original parchment has been in the Municipal Historical Museum since the middle of the last century and will be on display for an entire year. School classes from all over the city will come to see it, which, in my opinion, is very important. I believe it's essential to instill a sense of tradition in the younger generation. In addition, special events will be scheduled for the entire year and decorative posters and banners displayed everywhere. Every resident of the city with a valid identity card will receive a colorfully enameled pin depicting a silhouette of the town square and engraved with the words "One Thousand Years D." along with the dates.

Sometimes I think everyone in town knows me. Maybe it's because my name is often mentioned in the newspapers and on TV. Strangers sometimes say hello to me on the street. I suppose I do stand out because of my trademark wide-brimmed hat and red scarf. In the summer I usually wear a light silk scarf.

I had gone to the bank to pick up some cash as a deposit for the graphic artist who's designing the jubilee pins. I like to pay up front for projects related to the celebration because it cuts down on bureaucracy. I make sure I get signed receipts, and from time to time I hand them in at the Office of Financial Management so I can be reimbursed.

I inserted my cash-card into the automatic-teller and focused on my pin-number which is pretty easy to remember because it combines elements of my father's date of birth and the year I began school. I'm sure everyone concentrates on their pin-number when they punch it in on an automatic-teller. You can't afford to make mistakes. Naturally, I cup my hand over the number-pad when I'm typing in my pin. That's what they suggest in case criminals have set up a hidden camera to spy on you. I don't think anything like that has ever happened at our branch, but you never know, so I'm careful.

I always punch in the numbers without looking which is easy because the number-pad only has nine keys. This time too, but then I heard a dissonant buzz and saw a message blinking on the monitor in bold red letters: "Pin incorrect". That had never happened to me before, and so I tried once more, this time very attentively. But again It happened. That really surprised me, and, well, it scared me too. This all happened at lunchtime, when only the automatic-teller area of the bank was open. I've had my account there for twenty-five years and know most of the tellers. But no one was there, and that made me feel helpless.

I remembered reading somewhere that you only get three tries. After that, your card is swallowed by the machine. I didn't want to risk that, so I decided to return after the lunch hour. Still, the inconvenience was annoying.

On the way home (I live just a few blocks from the bank), I saw my neighbor Mrs. F. on the other side of the street. We always have a little chat when we run into each other. She's been alone a lot since her husband died. "Nobody has time for me", she'll tell me, so I always make an effort to spend a few minutes talking with her which is all the attention she wants anyway. I guess she didn't notice me from across the street.

I still had plenty of time till my appointment with the designer. Anyway, if push came to shove, I did have enough cash on hand to pay the deposit. But that would have left me with my wallet empty, which I don't like. It makes me feel too vulnerable.

My family is not originally from here, so being asked to join the organizing committee—even though I'm not "old blood" —was a great honor. Sure, I was born here, in the old maternity hospital downtown, in fact, which—sad to say—was closed a few years ago and moved to that new state of the arts medical complex at the edge of town. I loved that old building, the high ceilings, the arched hallways, the generous rooms with a view onto the garden. My children were born there too. Despite the protests, they turned it into a high-end shopping emporium. My grandfather settled here as a young man shortly after the War. Those were hard times, and he shouldered his load like everyone else, maybe even more so in fact, clearing streets of rubble, rebuilding half-standing buildings and laying the foundation for new ones. Later, he ran for a political office . . . and won.

I have no memory of him. He died right after I was born. When they named a street after him about twenty years ago, the whole family attended the ceremony. My father even held a speech. He wasn't much of a public speaker, and everyone could see that he was nervous. He died not long after that. No connection, I'm sure (ha ha). When people hear my name, they sometimes ask if I'm related to the person the street is named after. I'm always full of pride when I say yes, but I try not to show it. I don't want people to think it's gone to my head.

On the way home from the bank, it started to rain, though there was no rain in the forecast. It began as a harmless trickle and suddenly turned into a violent cloudburst. The sky was giving everything it had. Fortunately, I reached the entrance of my building before the worst of it. Still, I got wet.

When I'd left for the bank earlier, I'd noticed that there was mail, but when I opened the mailbox now, it was empty which was strange because my wife was still at work. I was sure there must be some explanation. I went up the steps fairly briskly. I rarely take the lift. My doctor says that climbing stairs is good for my knees and my heart. When I turned the key, I saw that the lock was unbolted, which made me wonder if I'd forgotten to lock the door. But that would have been a first. Or maybe my wife was home which would also explain why the mailbox was empty.

I opened the door and saw the lights were on, but I didn't remember leaving them on. And another thing: everything looked tidy. To be honest, my wife and I are not the most orderly people. I called out her name, but then a stranger, an attractive woman, trim, thirtyish maybe, a total stranger, peeked around the corner and said hello in a very friendly way.

Before I managed to ask who she was, she was already tugging at my wet jacket, insisting I let her slip it off, which I did. Then she took my hat and scarf and disappeared with them. When she returned, she was still smiling. After that, she disappeared into the kitchen.

All this happened so quickly, I had no time to ask questions. I walked into the living room—it too was unusually tidy—and just sat in the rocking chair. Then I heard a beep, which startled me. It seemed to be coming from my shirt pocket. It was my phone of course. I had set the calendar alarm to remind me about my appointment with the man who was designing the jubilee pins. At that moment it occurred to me that I shouldn't forget to take along the draft I'd sketched which I'd left on my desk. I wanted him to have a look at it. It would really have pleased me if he used any of my ideas.

I got up from the rocking chair and went to my study, still nonplussed by the tidiness and brightness in the apartment, but the draft wasn't on my desk. I was sure I'd left it there. In fact, it looked like someone had straightened up the desktop totally. That irritated me, and that's when I marched off into the kitchen to get to the bottom of all this.

"Do you know where my sketch for the commemorative pin is?" I asked the woman.

She smiled but didn't answer.

"I have an appointment with the designer today. I need that sketch."

She just kept smiling, and then she said, "Come, sit down at the dining-room table. I'll bring you something to drink. How about some fennel tea?"

It surprised me that she knew I liked fennel tea, especially in the winter—and it was winter, something I may have forgotten to mention. I nodded and went off obediently into the dining room and sat down at my usual place. That's when I noticed that my puzzle was gone. I always have a small puzzle on the table to tinker with while waiting for dinner (not that my wife does all the cooking; sometimes I cook too). I enjoy the challenge of a good puzzle. But the clutter was gone and my puzzle too.

"Have you seen my puzzle?" I asked the woman when she came in with my tea along with a small platter of shortbread cookies—my favorites.

But she just smiled. "There you go," she said.

"My puzzle. Have you seen my puzzle?" I repeated, trying my best to conceal my impatience.

That's when her expression turned serious. "I'm afraid I don't understand," she said.

Those words hurt, I'm not sure why, and I echoed them sarcastically: "I'm afraid, I don't understand!"

I guess that reaction startled her. She left the room without a word.

It occurred to me that I should have said, "Listen, I was born here . . . in the old maternity hospital. There's a street in this town named after my grandfather, and I'm on the planning committee for the thousand year anniversary of the founding of our city . . . and furthermore, *I* . . . understand . . . *you*!" Instead I just drank my tea, ate a couple of shortbread cookies and decided to postpone any other decisions till later.

I really didn't want to hurt her feelings, and I was sorry if I had. Anyway, I was sure there was a logical explanation to this misunderstanding. Everything has an explanation. I got up from the table and went looking for her to apologize. She was in the bedroom changing her blouse. Why she was doing that in the middle of the day was beyond me. In my opinion, she was already smartly dressed. She was standing there, her shoulders bare, in her undergarments.

I wanted to turn my eyes away but couldn't. "I just want to apologize for being so . . . impatient," I said, eyeing her in a conciliatory manner. Then it crossed my mind that maybe she still didn't understand me because she didn't respond. We both just smiled, and I returned to the rocking chair and just rocked for a while . . .

. . . that is, till my phone started buzzing again. I knew it was another reminder about my appointment which was going to take place in an hour. I got up and stepped over to the window and saw that it had stopped raining. In fact, it was sunny out, just like the weather report had forecast, which is why that cloudburst puzzled me. I was sure there must be some explanation.

By now the bank was definitely open, and I wanted to return there, hoping to run into the blond teller. I've known her for years (she began wearing glasses recently). I was positive she could resolve the problem. I didn't want to risk having my bankcard swallowed by the automatic-teller. Especially because I only had one more chance.

Once again I went to my study. I still couldn't understand why everything looked so orderly. At least my bookshelves were still there—and as full of books as ever. But then I took a closer look and saw that those were not my books. There were lots of interesting books, but they weren't mine. That irked me tremendously. I like my books, and I'm proud to say that I have read more than half of them and I still intended to read the rest.

I began searching for my sketch again, this time, everywhere—even on the bookshelves and briefly in the drawers. So much was unfamiliar. Unfamiliar is the wrong word. I did see familiar things too—I mean apart from the furniture—even some book titles, but, still, they were not *my* books.

I thought of asking the woman about the books. I was convinced that she held the key to all this. But I was afraid she wouldn't understand me. But why shouldn't she? As far as I could determine, we were speaking the same language? Then it occurred to me to call my wife who was most probably still at work. Odd that I didn't think of that before. Besides, I needed to prepare her for what to expect when she got home. That's when it occurred to me that the screensaver on my phone was an exact replica of the sketch I wanted to bring the designer. Well, not completely. Mine was a rough draft; this one was perfectly executed. Had someone taken my idea? Things like that happen. Maybe the woman had given my sketch to the committee, which would explain why I couldn't find it. I was confident there was a logical explanation and intended to look into the matter once I reached my wife.

No answer. Maybe she's out for coffee or at a meeting. I never know what goes on at her office. Then I saw I'd received a text message. Maybe from my wife. No. It was from the designer.

"Let's reschedule," he wrote. "Am unable to meet today. Sorry."

I suppose I was both disappointed *and* relieved. Granted, I still wanted to ask him about that image on my screensaver. But at least I didn't have to rush. I've never liked having to race against the clock.

I returned to my study intending to finally sort all this out. For some odd reason, that business with the screensaver especially bothered me. But who knows? The answer might turn out to be ridiculously easy. Maybe someone else on the committee had had the same idea. I mean, things like that *do* happen. I once read something about coincidences, that the same event can occur simultaneously at two places in the universe as if they were synchronized. I don't really understand what that means. Still, it does happen that two people sometimes have the same idea, maybe even in the same place and at the same time—or, at least almost at the same time. Anyway, how many ways are there to sketch a town square, add a slogan and a date? But none of this alleviated my irritation that my draft was missing. I decided now to check the desk drawers more thoroughly, and I was no longer in a hurry.

Well, the drawers were *not* as tidy as the rest of the apartment. I rummaged through masses of pencils and pens, knickknacks and trinkets, letters (addressed to someone I didn't know—but at my address!). There were pocket-knives, loads of them, old coins, paperclips, rubber-bands and photographs, lots of photographs, mainly of people I didn't know. Well, not entirely, because there were also photos of me there! Typical snapshots of me wearing my trademark hat and red scarf and taken at various venues: social events, in the park, on the street. some with my wife too, sometimes with neighbors and friends. For the life of me I couldn't recall when they had been taken. There were also photos of the woman, in fact, more of her than of me. And, in some of them, well, she was wearing nothing! In a few you could see her in some very compromising positions, sometimes with a good-looking young man, always the same man. At least in some pictures he had his clothes on. But why would anyone put pictures like those into my desk drawer?

At any rate, my sketch was nowhere. Then it occurred to me to call the chairman of the planning committee. Maybe he knew something. Unfortunately, I didn't have his private number. I had once written it on the back of an envelope and left it on my desk. No need to explain why it was useless to look for it there.

I was back in the rocking chair, leafing through a coffee-table book I didn't remember owning . . . unless my wife had bought it and never mentioned it. She sometimes does that. It was about chocolate—everything you've ever wanted to know about chocolate: Aztec recipes, the introduction of chocolate to Europe in the seventeenth century, conching, admixtures and preparation, manufacturers, specific exotic niche products. You name it. Being a chocaholic myself, I could easily imagine a book like that in our library. But as interesting as it was, I couldn't concentrate on it. Something was not right, but I couldn't figure out what. Another attempt to reach my wife. No answer. Then I heard rustling at the front door and thought, aha! It's her. Things like that happen. You think about something, and *voilà*! Synchronicity! I called out her name. But it wasn't her. I heard a man's voice, and the woman was talking with him in the hall. When he entered the living room, I recognized him as the person in the photos. He was smiling. I liked his face. Something sympathetic about it. I stood up and extended my hand, but he ignored the gesture and crunched me in his arms. We were standing face to face. He said something about the weather, about how he'd had a long day. I said something in return but was not convinced he'd understood. I didn't make an issue though. Everything is the same but different, I wanted to say but I thought, maybe I'll tell him that later. He and the woman were having a conversation about something, but I stopped listening pretty quickly. Then he disappeared into my study, and I returned to the rocking chair. I was curious what he was doing in my study, but I stayed put. I can't explain why.

We sat down to dinner. At least there was no competition for my seat and sitting there was about the most natural thing I'd experienced the whole day—except for the fact that my puzzle was missing.

They were talking about a picnic. I didn't catch whether it had taken place or was going to. That shows you how interested I was in their conversation. It's not as if they were ignoring me. They did make an effort to include me. Still, something was bothering me. I just couldn't put my finger on it. I was going to bring up the issue of the photos in the desk drawer, but I decided not to. Not just because they might not understand me. I also didn't want to embarrass them for obvious reasons.

Maybe I could have made some smalltalk about the cruise my wife was planning for us which, frankly, I wasn't looking forward to. She loves traveling. I'm a homebody. Besides, the jubilee has been keeping me pretty occupied these days. My wife is less interested in it—despite the fact that her family goes back many generations. Sometimes, I think that maybe I had been asked to join the planning committee not because of my grandfather's service to the city but because of my wife's long pedigree. On one occasion, I thought my wife might have insinuated that. It was on one of those days when we were not getting along. Happens in all marriages. At any rate, I made no effort to contribute to the conversation at the dinner table, and no one seemed to expect me to say anything.

By the way, dinner was fantastic. Have you ever had romaine salad with mango, tomato and caraway seeds? Well, I hadn't. And with a shot of apple-balsamico vinegar to round it out. Really tasty. After dinner, without asking, the woman brought me a fennel tea. It was as if she were reading my mind.

After dinner we watched TV—which I usually find boring. I hardly turn the TV on except to watch the news. I tried reaching my wife again, but there was no answer which led me to believe that maybe I had forgotten something. I mean, maybe she was on a business trip or something like that, and it had slipped my mind. Things like that happen. Sometimes my wife accuses me of being forgetful, which is strange, because I sometimes have the feeling that she's the one who's forgetful. But maybe I did forget something.

I started feeling tired and headed off to bed. I'm not sure if I said good night, and if I did, they probably didn't respond. I was getting used to not being understood. I washed, then went into the bedroom where I undressed and climbed into bed. My side is on the right, which is where I have my books, my radio, and, of course, a collection of puzzles. I'm a voracious puzzler. You name it, I have it: puzzles with pieces you have to join or separate, labyrinths, electronic puzzles, sudokos—even chess problems. Everything but crossword puzzles. They were never my thing. I've always enjoyed cozying up with a puzzle after a long day and mulling over it—looking for the hidden logic—until I solve it or am too tired to think. Then I shut the light and am out right away. But my puzzles were gone. In fact, my side of the bed was as tidy as the rest of the apartment. No books, no radio, no puzzles. Nothing but an alarm clock and a lamp on the night table. Pretty boring. I shut the light and began pondering over the events of this day as if *I* had become a puzzle I couldn't solve!

Not much time for contemplating though, because after a few minutes, they joined me in bed—and they really took up a lot of space. He was next to me, at least at the beginning, because then it seemed like they were all over the place—I mean in the bed. The lights were out, so I couldn't see what they were doing. It sounded like a wrestling match, and they were not particularly quiet. God knows how long it went on. At some point, they must have gotten tired, and so had I. I suppose we all fell asleep. At any rate, I never managed to get back to mulling over the events of the day.

When I woke up in the morning, I felt refreshed. It was light in the room. They were already gone, and I had the whole bed to myself, which I didn't mind, though it would have been nicer to have had a radio on the night table. I like listening to the news first thing in the morning. I have an ear plug connected to the radio so I can listen without disturbing my wife. Under the circumstances I had no reason to lounge in bed. I got up for my morning wash. The door to the bath was shut. I knocked, but there was no answer, which made me think no one was in there. I opened the door. They *were* in there and standing under the shower in a, well, very intimate way.

"Oh, excuse me," I said.

When they saw me, they chimed, "Good morning! Did you sleep well?"

I answered yes but couldn't tell if they'd gotten the message. I guess that irritated me, but I didn't complain. Actually, I did think of saying something. I just couldn't put it into words.

Then I remembered that I wanted to go to the bank after breakfast and ask the blond teller about my bankcard. I certainly didn't want to risk inserting it into the automatic-teller a third time. After all, if my pin still didn't work, it might make matters even worse.

JOHN PATRICK HIGGINS

The Casual Ghost

There is a piece of paper Blu Tacked to a pillar about ten feet away, and it does my job better than me.

It says: "Tables 4–8 this way." And I can't say that. I'm not that precise. There's too much of me in the way. I'm a smear on glass, fuzzying everything up.

I'm a casual host, standing on the concourse of an Arts institution, wearing company-issue slacks with the creases built in. The trousers have had a previous owner. Over my left nipple is a badge that tells people "My Name Is Irwin" (my name is not Irwin).

When the snooker's on, I stand here and smile at the day drinkers gambling on their phones. Occasionally, I ask if I can help and they look confused, until they realize I'm attempting to direct them somewhere or trying to maximise their cultural experience. I'm not telling them when to shout "Housey Housey" on the Sun Bingo app.

I can't think on my feet, so I'm not good at this job. The work involves seas of boredom, swathes of unvarying tedium. It's hypnotically uninteresting. Your mind reels from inactivity, it rebels. You enter a liminal world, one foot to the left of the space you're staring into. Somebody asking you a question at that point is traumatic, snapping you back into disappointing reality. You gabble, jabber, stutter. The sign, exemplary, gummed to its pillar, has none of these problems. It's a limpid pool. It doesn't need you to like it, it doesn't need to impress you, and it doesn't want to go the extra mile. I envy its completeness. It's unchanging, where I'm a storm on desert sands, though you wouldn't know it to look at me, grinning in my corporate shirt, blurting out local information to unhurried passers-by.

It's just a sign. It has words and an arrow on it. It isn't masquerading as Irwin or unsure whether the restaurant is open today (it is).

I remember school trips to museums before museums were child friendly and interactive. Nowadays, you can ride a dinosaur, split an atom or experience what it's like to be a sneeze, but when I was young, museums were damp, clattering Victorian institutions, full of green glass cases of igneous rocks, stuffed fish, or the remains of some hapless pachyderm, immortalised on the pointy end of a Cro-Magnon spear. All of it labelled in boilerplate Latin, on a brass plaque screwed into a marble plinth. Next to these, living fossils themselves, were the museum guards, straining their uniforms, hair stiff with pomade under concierge caps. They sat there: ex -army, shrapnel always on manoeuvres, glowering at children who didn't want to be there.

I used to wonder about them, about their Bakelite specs and blue, pannier jowls. Was this it for them? Sitting amongst the dead, staring down at the living? After everything they'd seen: the wars, the foreign soil stuck to their boots, all that heavy past. I thought of the men they'd killed, the women they'd failed to satisfy, only to end their days here, amongst threadbare tapirs, crumbling papyrus, dead currency. How could they do that to themselves?

But it's what I've done.

The uniform's a bit more casual. There's less marble and Latin and more natural light. There are snacks and refreshments available in the foyer, and two bars on the third and fifth floor (though only the third-floor bar is open today). The colour scheme suggests corporate positivity, and I am obliged to smile at people when I direct them. But it's the same job. I sit there. Or I stand. I pace, back and forth, like a zoo animal losing its wits.

Today I have been advising people on the location of the nearest toilet. That was what was on the rota: "Comfort Guide." On a couple of occasions, I've had to run after the clients them as they sail past the clearly advertised toilet door and wandered into the VIP lounge (currently inactive).

I scurry after them, crying "Sir! Sir!" They are all male. The snooker is on.

Perhaps that's why they do it. Everyone likes to be called "sir". Before this job, I don't think I'd called anyone "sir" since school, but it comes naturally now, as though I actual enjoy the loss of status. There *is* a part of me that finds something exhilarating in boredom, in wasted time, in squandered effort. Something giddily exciting about a fat man in tracksuit bottoms ignoring my accurate toilet directions. It's like a cosmic truth laid out in front of me: proof, finally, of my insignificance, my lack of worth, my place in the scheme of things. I relish the abasement. I deserve this.

So, how may I optimise your experience today?

Jason Graff

Sadness Machine

Nothing so validated the couple's sense of taste as the look contractors gave them when they attempted to describe the house they'd always envisioned. *Think Richard Serra*, they would say to an ever-changing, yet remarkably similar cast of balding, thick set characters sporting packs of smokes in the front pockets of their shirts and pencils tucked behind their ears. These men all wore the same befuddled look that only grew more fuddled as the couple went on to explain what they meant. The card-thin walls would be perfect except when it was really cold or really hot. It would be a showplace as much as a house.

Dream house or no, the woman wasn't sure how much longer she would be happy with the man. He hadn't done anything wrong; she was just always sure that hers was a restless heart. This was how she thought of herself all her adult life, despite how settled and conventional she'd always been. Someone craving excitement had to be living inside of her; she just knew it.

Fighting often, their three sons were careful not to break things when it got rough. There were some ground rules they all tacitly agreed to. First among them, no slamming each other up against the walls.

Sometimes his boys felt like strangers to the man. He wanted to get to know them, but they seemed more distant the older they grew. It was the opposite of how he felt about his years with the woman. She knew him, of that he was sure. Not only that, but he was certain that she cherished this knowledge above all things. It wasn't that he thought himself especially hard to know or rich or complex, but he took for granted the idea that anyone would cherish knowing about something so completely; like expert beekeepers or heart surgeons or the guy who used to fix the fountains at the mall.

Sometimes the woman lamented the waning of their sex life. She considered plastic surgery to become again the object of her man's desire. He could hardly keep his hands to himself when they'd first met. But would it be enough? Would his desiring her again in such an animalistic way renew her feelings for him? She never thought herself the type of person who would even entertain such questions, see herself in such a way.

The Jack of Diamonds went missing from the dining room, which was made entirely of face cards. Eating was one activity the woman didn't mind feeling as though she was being watched while she did it. There were no face cards in their bedroom or ensuite, and she avoided the bathroom on the first level because of the king in the wall. A breeze blew the placemats off the table and sent tumbleweeds of cat hair rolling across the floor. It had been some time since she'd seen the cat and wondered where it was. She called around trying to find someone who could fix the house. *Think Richard Serra*, she told each of them.

The man was troubled by things at work. The money was still as good as ever, better even, but he'd rather inconveniently developed a real curiosity about what his company did. He stayed late for a couple of weeks to go over the latest R&D documents. What he learned kept him up at night.

Your worries are my worries, the woman told him and listened to him agonize about what she wasn't sure. She liked the money too but her job paid enough to support them. She meant to mention this each time he started up, clearing his throat into his pillow then rolling over with a *Hun...*, but she felt like he just needed someone to listen. They'd reached the point, after all their years together, when one felt they could tell when the other simply wanted to be heard.

The cat died outside in the garden. By the time one of the boys discovered the corpse, it barely resembled the pet that they all liked well enough, though no one really loved. Still, they had a kind of service for him and a burial. One of the twins cried and then, once he was finished, the other started up. They were still boys. The woman held them both and thought it a pretty good day. It had been some time since she'd felt so much like a mom.

When a nine of clubs went missing from the shared upstairs bathroom, the couple began to suspect one of the boys was playing tricks. None of the three had been too happy with the new house, though all seemed to have settled into it once the place was finished. They checked the boys' rooms one day when they were all out. In the twins' room, they found one had turned all of his clothes inside out but no playing cards, at least none big enough to be a wall. In their eldest's, they found two dozen jars of yellow mustard under his bed but no cards at all. Their discoveries seemed worth discussing with the children, but the couple couldn't think of a way of bringing the subjects up without revealing they'd been snooping. *Let's keep a closer eye on them*, the man said.

One day, it rained hard enough to make the cards soggy, but the house held up. There were some puddles on the floor that they made the boys clean them up. They did so, though it didn't seem like they enjoyed it. Not that that was required.

What is it? she asked when he brought that awful black cube home. *It has a technical term but really it's a sadness machine*, the man said. *Don't worry, we'll keep it away from the kids. The people that would use it the most is who I'm saving from this thing*, he said. All the phrases he'd recited but not yet lived.

Is this from work? Is this what's been keeping you up? the woman asked. *I'm hungry*, the man said, *I could go for some celery with cream cheese and bacon*. He always tried to distract her with snack options that sounded unappetizing, usually, but not always, involving cream cheese.

A few days after the storm, once the walls had dried, the twins noticed some were bowing badly, allowing air to enter along the sides. It was a cool wind, warmed only by the neighbors' gossip. So the woman began calling contractors again. *Think Richard Serra*.

The Wifi password for the house was changed to Ultimatefrisbee69. One of the twins did it as a joke but regretted it when the rest just went along. In time, he found he could no longer even search for Ultimate Frisbee-themed pornography. And how else do you become a man?

The eldest finally got accepted to college. It was a good distance from home. Everyone was relieved; the man and the woman because they feared with his poor grades, lack of extracurriculars and general body odor that he wouldn't get into a decent school. The twins loved their brother but loved the thought of having their own rooms more.

Now, the other twin was wearing his clothes inside out too. Neither the man nor woman noticed at first. When they finally said something, he acted like it had been going on for a while and was no big deal. *Let's keep an eye on him,* the man said. Anything to avoid a confrontation.

No one else in the family knew but the man's father had been very confrontational, getting in his face over the smallest things, ever since he was a small boy; a face that went red with eyes bulging from his head, veins rising to the top layer of his skin as they carried discourteous blood to and from his heart. It was a face the man still pictured when he talked to his father on the phone and that old gruffness came out.

They decided enough time had passed to get a new cat. The family was all set on saving an older, adult cat but none of the mature felines at the shelter seemed too anxious to leave. The man got scratched by one when he went to pick it up. So, they chose a kitten instead. They couldn't agree on a name so he was just Kitty, until the name kind of stuck. The man would look at the animal as it sat in his lap and wonder if that wasn't what had happened to Babe Ruth.

When it came time for the oldest to leave for college, he didn't want to go. He cried. He gnashed his teeth. He took the car keys and hid them. The twins were concerned. They tried talking to him. The woman tried. Even the man, with his hatred of emotions, especially sadness, and confrontation, especially between father and son, tried. No one could convince him. Later that night, as everyone else slept, the eldest took up his packed bags, walked down the street to the bus station and left. *On my way,* he texted them as a group.

The family discussed it the next morning and all agreed he'd simply come to his senses. No one wanted to embarrass him by forcing some sort of confession from him. He was just a kid the man and woman said. The twins agreed but hated this as it meant they were still kids as well. The man never let on but something about the whole incident nagged him, something he couldn't mention.

One day, when the others were out shopping, he moved some cards leaning against each other in the corner of his closet and checked on the sadness machine. He could see at once that it had been tampered with. He thought of calling the son now in college and talking to him about the machine, about ordering him to never tell his brothers about it, and then yelling at him for snooping. It was none of the boy's business what he kept in his closet. Even in just thinking that way, he could feel some of his father rise up in him, a red cherry flame of anger. He texted his son to ask him how it was going. *Fine,* came the reply three days later.

The woman went through another bout of considering the drooping flesh beneath her eyes and chin, the wrinkles like cracked arid land on her forehead. She did some investigating and found a plastic surgeon that was well regarded and not overly expensive. Pausing before she made a consultation appointment, she contemplated speaking with the man first, but simply decided it wasn't his face and then booked the appointment.

He came home that night and announced he'd been fired. As a way to make them both feel better, she seduced him as they readied for bed. She'd almost forgotten how to do it, but then it came easy. She lay in his arms after and for the first time in a long time, in years, thought: this is the man I could be with until I die. First thing the next morning, she canceled her appointment with the surgeon.

The man changed the Wifi password to thinkRichardSerra.

The twins got detention for accumulating too many tardies. *This is no way to start the year,* their mother told them and threatened to make them take the bus. They took it seriously and, moving forward, planned to shower at night to make certain they wouldn't be late. She liked how solution-oriented they'd proven to be, and no longer minded them wearing their clothes inside out. The man had been right to caution against confrontation. The problem had sorted itself out in the best way possible, by simply becoming a normal part of life and no longer a problem at all.

The eldest's first semester was going far better than anyone could have hoped. He wasn't sure he wanted to come home for Thanksgiving, but his family was excited to see him. He started several texts to his brothers to warn them about the black cube in their father's closet but never was able to send it. He wasn't sure he knew exactly what it was.

When he finally called to ask about it, his father told him about a cream cheese stuffing he was experimenting with for the Thanksgiving meal. *I'm doing more of the cooking since I've retired,* he said. The boy didn't realize his dad was even that old. He wondered if he'd missed a party or something.

One day they all came home from buying kitten food to find an unusually strong wind had blown the top of their house off. The twins wanted to move but their parents claimed they could all live downstairs for a while. They vowed to find someone who could fix the place up right. Trying to make a game of it, the woman promised an ice cream cone to whomever could pick up the most cards from the backyard. The man won easily because the boys didn't really even try.

Dan Tremaglio

Charioteer

The food court is a holy place. This I've known since I was the smallest patron of our nation's greatest mall. The options. The aromas. Pieces of pizza too big to be considered pieces. Walk from end to end with your hands folded behind you. Wait for hunger to assert its need. Escalate to a higher plane. Purchase a churro. Be redeemed.

But something happened at some point. I cannot say when. The mall lost its magic. Became desanctified. Eyes no longer guided upward. This basilica full of sneakers and plastic jewelry I once visited barefoot during the month of June. How did it happen?

Upon these matters I meditate while waiting at a modest roundtable in front of Phyllis' Corndogs. I've been waiting for well over an hour now, always early for my appointments. I am to be interviewed for a prestigious position which will result in a considerable surge of income and probably renown. Most of my problems will vanish instantaneously. The gentleman traveling from afar to interview me is a true potentate, an elite, a leader in his field and in other fields as well. He will be interviewing me to confirm what he already suspects, I suspect, that I am a kindred spirit, a long lost brother.

But the meeting is not to be. This I grasp in a flash of insight.

Dearest gods, the mistake I nearly made! Succumbing to plastic-packed temptation! Electing the ephemeral over the eternal! Applying for a job!

No, I cannot deny for one more second where my true path must lie! Now I must hurry to make up for lost time.

Without panic, I retrieve my aunt's cellphone and summon a car. The mall remains consecrated ground after all, which means cars tarry outside and I am picked up in minutes.

"The narrow road to the deep north," I reply when asked to clarify my destination.

"You mean I-5?" my driver asks, a black-haired man who does not turn to speak. The app identifies him as one Jagannath Krishnahari.

"An archer won't presume to tell a charioteer of chariot business," I joke, ever ready to cut through awkwardness with bonhomie and wit. This social skill of mine is one of many abilities the potentate wished to witness firsthand. He will be disappointed, no doubt, which saddens me. Disappointing potent persons is not something I enjoy. Nonetheless, I have been called, am choiceless, summons-bound.

"Fine," my driver says, and off we glide on an electric wave.

Our itinerary will be long and arduous and involve numerous waystations. I regret not undertaking this journey in profound solitude as so many pilgrims have before me, but I am humble enough to understand that one cannot suffer such a quest alone. Humility is another trait I'd been poised to present mid-interview. Indeed the potentate must be a highly humble man himself, which is why he sought me out in the first place. He would know even great men require company during daring exploits. I am very pleased with this new insight and wish to share it.

"I need you," I tell my driver.

Despite his black hair and dark complexion, my driver has very bright blue eyes. This I note when our gazes meet in the rearview mirror, a look of concern on his side. Perhaps he feels unworthy of praise, an estimable chap who struggles with self-esteem as so many do. Perhaps he is new to this land where he makes his trade shuttling pilgrims from past to future. I refrain from informing him that it cannot be by chance alone he heeded my aunt's cellphone's summons. We will wait for the inevitable discussion of fate to come.

Hours later we stop at a station to zap lithiums for the car. My driver does not ask me to pump. I'd been planning to take on some of these logistical tasks, a gesture that would confirm me as a man of both tower and street, of library and tavern, traits the potentate would have sensed in me immediately. My driver deprives me of the chance by not asking. This is probably for the best, for I am so consumed with philosophical preoccupations I scarcely notice we have stopped until the charge is through.

The hour is past midnight when we stop at a popular chain of inn for whom I do not wish to advertise and so will leave nameless. My driver books us separate rooms under my aunt's account, though I confess I never even visit mine, instead passing the night deep in thought in the little lobby bar.

So much has changed in so narrow a window, I reflect. Early this morning one clear defined path stretched out before me. An epiphany in a food court later and that path is gone, replaced by the usual wild winding one that fades before long into fog. Why did I opt for this? A role had been reserved for me, one of decoration and acclaim, yet once again I forsook the tangible in favor of the formless, certain that the role that can be taken up is not the eternal role. When oh when, I wonder for the ten thousandth time, must we trade uncut wholeness for something easier to carry around in a pocket over our heart, a word written on a scrap of paper with a pen running out of ink? Today was the day I had prepared for just such a trade, a merchant's morning fit for riding an escalator slowly down from the sacred to the secular, but all that vanished in an instant at a sticky table which wobbled beneath my elbows.

My revelry is so soul-consuming I do not notice the sunlight bending through my empty glass, nor do I hear the bustle of early morning hotel happenings.

"Car's ready," my driver says beside me, an overnight bag in hand. His hair is damp and combed and he wears a fresh shirt and smiles politely. He appears well rested, precisely the trait one hopes for in such a man.

Off we go. All morning we continue our journey along the very thoroughfare we logged a dozen hours upon yesterday. "When will ever this road terminate?" I wonder.

"I-5 turns into 55 eventually," my driver tells me.

"Fascinating. The path perpetuates but under another name. Is it the same road then?"

His fine eyebrows furrow in the mirror. "I don't know about that. It'll be the same, and it'll be different."

I laugh heartily. Why is the examining soul moved most by paradox? What use is such thinking? How can it be applied? These are questions I expected to address during my interview, wherein I was prepared to argue for the first time in favor of the concrete, in favor of the quote-unquote objective, the quote-unquote real. But from that interview I have fled. Do I regret it? No! Yet I cannot deny that the challenge I have taken up in its stead is fey and nebulous and likely doomed for failure. Despair rears its scaly head.

"Will we be stopping for lunch?" my driver asks me.

I am about to decline when I acknowledge my drool. Yes, I am drooling. Apparently the mention of food alone elicits a Pavlovian response, which is hardly puzzling, considering my previous meal was some 48 hours ago.

"Fine idea," I tell him. "Feel free to pull over at the next place you deem sufficient."

He does exactly that at rest stop situated along a promontory overlooking a wooded slope that dives down toward the ocean. The water is grey near the shore and shrouded farther out by a curtain of rain being dragged north by fast pale clouds. A picnic table is positioned for appreciating the vista and we seat ourselves along its westward facing side. Together we dine on a wedge of cheese my driver produces from his travel bag, also a bottle of water, a bag of almonds, and two plums a piece. Three low-flying drones pass below us in a V, heading back the way we came.

"How are you keeping?" my driver asks me when we have finished our lunch. "Still planning to push on?"

"Naturally. How much longer do you expect the trip to take, given our current pace?"

"One more day to the port, then another day or so at sea. That will put us on the far shore. Once there, it won't be much longer. Or not in the conventional sense. The roads over there are . . . different."

"Very good. I feel eager."

My driver smiles. His eyes are still aimed at the offing when he says, "Can I ask you something?"

I know what he will say, so I say it for him. "What do I hope to find at the end of this odyssey? A fair question, one I wish I could answer with a single sentence or couplet at a table overlooking the ocean. I'm afraid I must disappoint you."

My driver chuckles. "Men smarter than me have said it's the journey that matters in the end, not the destination. I won't argue. There is one thing I've decided though, and that is without a destination, there is no journey at all. Without a destination, it's just running away."

Chills crackle across me. Suddenly I wonder whether my driver is a driver at all and not something more. I've always been a believer in the hooded god, the king disguised as commoner. How proper would it be if my driver was actually a blue-eyed avatar incognito, the embodied cosmic source of all that is, which he could prove by allowing his head to explode, returning temporarily above the shoulders to an undifferentiated state wherein his ears are not ears and his eyes are not eyes but a trillion planets revolving about a billion stars in the outers arm of a million milky way galaxies that spin like the brain of that charioteer in the poem my aunt read when I stayed home sick one time long ago even though I was not sick at all or not sick in the bodily sense but simply lying like we all do in the navel of a slumbering creator who dreams the dream of all that is and was and will be and won't?

My driver collects the four plum pits, places them in the now almond-less sack before rewrapping the cheese, screwing the cap back on the water, and packing these away in his travel bag. "I'll check tomorrow's ferry schedule," he says, then rises from the table.

Prometheus means foresight, I remember.

The highway is empty for the rest of the afternoon. Around sundown I-5 changes its name to 55 or else ceases to be and is replaced or both or neither. When we pull into a station after dark I insist on zapping lithiums myself. My driver makes a call.

The next day is grey but warm, the air still and silent, when we pull into port. My driver conveys our reservation to a ferry official who takes our coins and guides us with yellow flags into the belly of a great steel ship. Once parked, we leave the car and climb a narrow stairwell and step out onto the slippery upper deck. Our hands on the railing, we look back over the land we have just left, watching the waiting cars being ushered onboard below, the shouted directions of ferry officials echoing in the hold.

Soon the moorings are thrown and our vessel embarks at the appointed hour. Then the coast is gone and we are enveloped on all sides by calm open ocean, by the rhythmic roll of infinite flux as the ship's reactors purr beneath our feet, ferrying us from one land mass to another, from this body to the next.

Invisible Illness Dress-Up
chronic pain
joint pain
migraine ~ head aches
emotional baggage
arthritis
dizziness
fatigue ~ exhaustion
throat issues
Sweating ~ fevers

David Rose

LINNAEUS—A LIFE

"The system is not so much the point of departure as the element in which arguments have their life."
Wittgenstein.

He picks up a stone, round, granular, strokes it with his fingers, his lips, and, into his mouth, his tongue.

—Carl, take that out at once. You may swallow it.

—Look, Mama has plucked you a flower.

He takes it from her, feathers it against his cheek. It is soft as the down of her arm. It smells not unlike her after a bath. It tickles him as she does.

—What is it called, Mama?

—I don't know. Ask Papa.

—What is it called, Papa?

—Scabious.

—That is a horrid name.

—That is what it is called.

—I don't care for that name. I shall call it something else.

He holds the flower closer, staring, willing. He presses the mute flower against the stone, harder, harder, until it is crushed. Stamping his foot, he hurls the stone far into the shrubbery.

*

A soft day in early spring, the breeze rumpling the turf. He falls to his knees at a cleft in the outcrop, bends to the flower as it bends in the wind, petals bragging open, the colour of sky. He runs the back of his fingers along the silverspined leaves, dislodging the last of the dew.

The blue prisms with his tears, then his fingers are scrabbling into the cleft, fumbling for the root.

Defeated, he pulls the flower from its nest of foliage and puts it carefully into his shirt.

The day is warm and he is far from home.

In the hush of his room, he fills a jug with water and unbuttons his shirt. The flower has faded, the petals are limp, one torn. The tears well up in an orgy of rage.

*

Dropping the book, he gets to his feet and crosses the garden. Out onto the road, he walks, faster and faster, rolling the names around his mouth.

Faster and faster, until he is running, flailing his arms, with no relief.

He stands, his mouth dry, under a tree.

He is startled from his melancholy by a glancing blow from a falling walnut. He picks it up, squeezes it, then dropping it, cracks it with his heel. Splitting the carapace, he eases out the nut. It lies in his hand, glistening, newly hatched.

He chews it slowly, swallows it carefully.

He walks homeward, names welling up into his throat, new names, unheard-of names, moist and glistening.

He stamps, tramps home, chanting, spitting out the names like stones.

*

He dismembers the pile of books, one by one. The last book of the pile he opens, takes out the pressed flowers and lays them on his bed. He leans, breathes over them, the names settling like dew.

*

Mama is terribly upset at my choice of vocation. She says our place is to praise God in our allotted task, as the flowers do in theirs. I told her my mission is to seek out the task of flowers in the Grand Design. There is more to Nature than feathery leaves and gaudy colours. Papa supports me, at least......

*

He sits, looking through the window. A ladybird lands on the pane, outside. He watches as it scurries purposefully about. He traces its journey with his finger, from inside, moving as it moves; a slow, slurred figure-of-eight, a half-circle to the east, a turn to southwest.

He seeks the pattern in its progress, to predict its path. It moves on, eccentrically, antennae trembling.

Defeated, he taps the glass against its body. Heedless, it moves on. He taps again, harder and again, until the glass cracks and spiders.

*

A warm day in May. With picnic basket and notebook he walks into the woods. He divests himself of coat and vest and sits down in the sun.

He is woken by a prick beneath his sleeve, followed by a pulsing itch. He pulls the sleeve up to reveal the epicentre of the throb. It swells as he watches. He is curious, furious, and in pain. He searches his limbs for the culprit, then the undergrowth. On hand and knees he gropes around, until his arm is found by a stand of nettles and he is forced to withdraw.

Picking up the picnic basket in his teeth, he sees a tiny thread-like worm, knotting in the sun. He rolls it into the basket, to study and exact revenge.

*

I have made the most astounding and fruitful discovery; concerning the part played by the pistils and stamens in the sexual act of pollination.

For do you not see? A method presents itself of organizing the floral kingdom! By counting the stamens and pistils, plants may be consigned to a limited number of classes; after which, by study of the characters of the genera within each class, plants may be placed in their correct genus.

Using this system to advantage enables us to throw a net over nature and bring it to order........

*

The day was fine and warm, with a light and cooling western breeze. As the forest grew more dense, the sweet lark sang no more; but the song-thrush welcomed us from the fir-tops.

Beyond Gävle, I came upon quantities of a lowly but charming plant with a myriad nodding heads. I have since identified it as *Campanula serpyllifolia*—the name given it by Bauhin, but which I regard as inapt. I am musing on something more suitable.

*

Have become much preoccupied with teeth and teats. Were I able to know how many teeth and of what kind every animal had, how many teats and where placed, I should be able to devise a system for the arrangement of all quadrupeds.

I find myself looking, at every opportunity, into mouths and under bellies. The Lapps seem not to take offence.

As to the taking of offence, I am indeed guilty, and without cause. My guide informed me that I had been referred to as a castrated reindeer, at which I took umbrage. He explained, however, that it is the Lapps' highest term of approbation.

This I now understand, since the reindeer is their entire provider, and the gelded animal the choicest. The reindeer provides their milk, their thread, their leather, their shelter and transport. So completely are their needs catered for that I was able to offer them nothing of any use. They rejected, politely, my snuff box, a pencil, and my second-best wig.

They remain self-sufficient, whilst I am an intrusion. Good-natured but curious, they........

*

He drops to his knees on the marshy ground and cradles the shrublet in his hand. With his pocket-knife he severs a sprig for inspection. He pronounces his identification. *Chamaedaphne.* The word is rough to his tongue, misshapen, soft and jagged. He spits it out.

Breathing slowly, he salivates, willing his lips, his larynx, as he strokes the sprig. Nothing comes. He breaks off a leaf, rubs it between his fingers. Still nothing. He breaks another leaf, touches it to his tongue as a burning coal, waits.

In desperation he clatters together the Greek counters: *ammos* (his fingers sandy from the leaves)—*ammoi, ammobyron, ammoanthus, ammokalos, kaloammos, anthokalos:* they are gravel in his mouth.

He gets to his feet, brushes off the caked and clinging mud, and limps impotently away.

*

He enters the room, stifling his heels, muffling his breath. Lilies cloy the camphor. He bends over the trestle.

He runs the back of his fingers over the pebbled knuckles, the petrified nose. He takes a skein of hair, plaits it round his fingers and feathers it against his cheek.

The eyes, closed, are scabious blue

....an irreparable sense of loss which I am unable to comprehend. Mama is dead—I shall see her no more. That I understand and grieve, but beyond that, something is lost and I know not what...

*

Furia infernalis: a small, thread-like annelid; harmless.

*

My dearest, further to our conversation of the previous eve, allow me to clarify my position. I wish, categorically, to do you the honour of asking you to become my help and staff in life.

I stand before you poor and unprepossessing. Yet if God spares me to complete my task of tidying the cosmos, our life together may prove fruitful and pleasant.

Do you accept? I have nothing to offer you but immortality.

Yours in anticipation, C.

*

Dearest, am enclosing for your collection, a pressed flower, lowly but charming. I have the honour of having it share my name, indeed of it being named after me—*Linnaea borealis* (hitherto misnamed *Campanula serpyllifolia*). Treasure it.

My work goes ahead apace.

*

.....most agreeable winter in Leyden. Attended and participated in the meetings of the scientific club of which I had the honour of being president.

My lectures went down, I believe, well.

The Dutch are an excellent people, always ready to learn; hospitable and courteous. They...

*

My little corolla, I ache to be with you, to be man and wife. I trust you too are counting the days. Preparations are in hand for my journey home. I plan to make a short detour to Paris, possibly on to Germany, thence, possibly, to England, then to fly to you with all haste...

*

Have been extraordinarily blessed in the support I have been given: the Scot Lawson, the great Gronovius, have welcomed me, not to mention earlier benefactors.

Names to find plants for: Celsia, Rudbeckia, Lawsonia, Gronovia...

*

My dearest wife, how strange and comforting to call you that at last. Let me assure you that the vows we made I do not take lightly, and wish, in that regard, to draw your attention to the single Lily I left in your room, in case its significance escape you.. I trust not.

I see by the position of the book-mark in your copy of my Systema Naturae that you are indeed devouring my wedding gift to you, and now have, I am confident, a grasp of my Sexual System of the Plant Kingdom.

You will thus have readily taken the symbolism of my gesture. It was, my dear, a monandrian lily!

A fitting token of our marriage, the single stamen representing the one and solitary husband, united with, devoted to, you, my pistil.

*

The students quiet as Linnaeus arrives. They lay out their specimens on the desks. They stumble out the names as Linnaeus points in turn.

He bids them consider, most carefully, the meaning of the names, the relationship to the plants. "If names were arbitrary, they would not be remembered. They derive from the plants like pips from fruit."

Serried frowns. He elaborates.

"By a careful study of the plant, characteristics are ascertained. These call to mind the name. This is one of the triumphs of the Linnaean nomenclature."

He elaborates further, warming.

"Take the specimen here. Previously known, inappropriately, as *Chamaedaphne*, I have renamed it, with due regard to its nature, *Andromeda.*"

Frowns deepen. His smile stiffens.

"Had you first seen the little plant, as I did, in its natural setting and at the height of its beauty, you would readily understand the reference, to Andromeda of old. She was anchored far out in the marshy water, tethered to her tuft, threatened by sea-dragons—frogs and toads—her head bowed in grief; flowers rosy for a while, but growing ever paler..."

The stifled clearing of a throat stops him short.

The door bangs.

*

A spread table. Linnaeus at the head, Fru Linnaea opposite, the little Linnaei ranked around.

The plattered pastry is browned to straw, butter-glazed. At Linnaeus' first incision, a plume of steam and spurt of gravy. A second radial incision, then, carefully lifting the tile of pastry, he bends forward, squinting and sniffing.

—*Lepus cuniculus*, my dear? Splendid.

She nods and spoons out the vegetables. From a covered tureen she scoops a mulch of leaves and squats them onto his plate. Part-blanched, marbled and veined, they sog into the pie. He stares silently, distraught.

—What, my dear, is this?

—A vegetable, my dear, sent from abroad by an anonymous admirer.

—Anonymous?

—I know neither his name nor its, but he assures us it is quite edible and most nutritious.

He picks up a leaf between knife and fork, spreads and smooths it on his napkin and hurries to his study.

Returning to cold dinner and empty table, he dissects another leaf, cuts out the stalk, and chews experimentally, note-book at the ready.

*

....old and tired and weary of hazard. Yet my work gathers momentum. I am sending out my apostles to the corners of the world. I tremble for them, in the knowledge of the dangers they face. But whosoever dies for my sake will be richly rewarded...

*

"Linnaeus' mania for naming and renaming has thrown the whole of Nature into confusion and botanists into dismay."

"Who would have thought that bluebells, lilies and onions could be up to such immorality?"

*

It has been said that I set such store by the Sexual System because, as a young physician, I grew rich on the ailments of Venus.

But it is written, "'Vengeance is mine, I will repay,' says the Lord." I have no doubt He will do so, having observed many examples of such in the past; which examples I am compiling into a little book, the Nemesis Divina, though I have as yet no plans to publish.

*

Sigesbeckia: a small-flowered, unpleasantly odoured weed; named after botanist Johann Georg Siegesbeck.

*

My Dear Frau Tärnström, words cannot convey the sadness I feel on the death of your husband. He was a great and brave man, a sacrifice to Flora in his pursuit of species. I can, however, assure you that he did not die in vain, nor will he be forgotten, since I am naming in his honour the genus *Ternstroemia*. Wherever botanists meet, your husband will be remembered.

If there is any other way I can be of assistance, dear lady, do not hesitate. Yours, etc.

*

....labouring mightily, rewriting my autobiography in the third person, disdaining as I do any appearance of immodesty.

Yet I grow weary of the flattery of men, and of their activities. Humankind I find curioUs. They........

*

He pauses en route to his study, as he does each morning, hands clasping and unclasping behind his back.

On the topmost shelf of the china cabinet is a tea set, brought from China by a disciple, made to Linnaeus' commission, each piece decorated with Linnaea Borealis: leaf, flower, root.

It is dusted, daily, reverently, by Fru Linnaea.

He regrets, as he does each day, the colour differences between the pieces, the correct pink flowers of the originals, the incorrect red flowers of the replacements for those broken in transit.

He frowns, taps his foot, continues his progress to the study.

He locks the door, walks to his cabinets. He opens a drawer, selected on whim, bends low over the pressed dry plants, breathing deliberately.

He is disturbed, puzzled, by the sound through the study door—the sound of the slow, methodical smashing of tea-cups.

He straightens to listen. After several minutes, there is silence.

He bends again to his specimens. The names drop from his lips like pebbles.

Melissa McCarthy

This Is the Silence, This Is the Noise

. . . in August 2022, back from my beach holiday, I gave this report to the denizens of the Glue Factory, a weekly online salon organised by the writer David Collard. The audience rubbed in their sun cream as they listened to some riffs on Ahab, surf guitar, and the labyrinth of the ear . . .

I was thinking about the demise of Captain Ahab, on the third day of the chase, in Herman Melville's 1851 *Moby-Dick*. (I'm often thinking about *Moby-Dick*.) It happens, Ahab's death, in surprising silence, for one who's so given to ranting and roaring.

Ahab's in one of the boats, off the *Pequod*, harpoon in his grip, still chasing the whale though everything's sinking all around him. As Ishmael describes it:

> The harpoon was darted; the stricken whale flew forward; with igniting velocity the line ran through the groove; -ran foul. Ahab stooped to clear it; he did clear it; but the flying turn caught him round the neck, and voicelessly as Turkish mutes bowstring their victim, he was shot out of the boat, ere the crew knew he was gone.

The "tranced" crew with him in the boat look on in amazement before being sucked down by a vortex and all drowned, in turn.

I was interested in this simile that Melville uses: "voicelessly as Turkish mutes." The adverb is a little vague: technically it applies to Ahab as passive victim: "voicelessly he was shot out of the boat"—he has no time to even cry out as the suddenly taut rope catches his neck (like Isadora Duncan) and pulls him out. But in sentence structure it's also comparing him to the killer, likening Ahab to the mute Turkish assassin who says nothing as he wields his rope and garottes his (also silent?) victim. Ahab is both killer and killed, which is fitting for a whaler who dies getting the whale. But either way, he's (finally) silent.

Ahab's last declamation just before this is shouting at the whale, which he does while using another interesting metaphor: he compares his life and himself to the waves of the sea. He shouts:

> 'Ho, ho! from all your furthest bounds, pour ye now in, ye bold billows of my whole foregone life, and top this one piled comber of my death! Towards thee I roll, thou all-destroying but unconquering whale;'

I am the sea, says Ahab in his last gasp. I'm the billows, the combers, I am the wave. He's becoming one, first in his language, then straightaway in his material location, with the waves. So my proposition is that Ahab is a surfer. This is, after all, what's required or aimed for in surfing: oneness with, though a certain detachment from, the wave.

Staying within this category of surfers, I was looking, a couple of years ago, at the obituaries of Dick Dale. That's full-name Richard Anthony Monsour, guitarist, born 4th May 1937, died 16th March 2019. American guitar player, very popular, successful and rich enough in his prime to buy a mansion and populate it with pet tigers.

Dick Dale didn't like to tour; he'd play local clubs in California, or, before the release of his *Surfer's Choice* album in 1962, you'd have to tune in, on the radio, if you wanted to hear him.

He was given the epithet of "the King of Surf Guitar," with surf guitar, surf music (for the benefit of any high court judges in the audience) being a genre of rock'n'roll music, popular in the sixties. What is this exactly?

The *Encyclopedia of Surfing* (a foundational text by Matt Warshaw, 2003, also permanently updating at https://eos.surf) describes surf music as a "pulsating, reverb-heavy, "wet"-sounding instrumental form," with "a hammering guitar-pick attack on a single string while sliding the fret hand high to low."

When Dick Dale himself is asked, by *The Surfer* magazine in 2010, what he thinks surf music is, he answers:

> A: Well, what it is, is the meaning of the sounds of the waves—like the echo and the sounds of the tube when my finger would be in the wall and I could hear it go, "Chhhhhhhhhhh!" And I'd take my strings and go, "Weeeeeeer!" And then you get that rumble just before you're going to be flung over—you know—right before you're going to go over the fucking falls and get slammed down. That rumbling and all that stuff like that they associated the heavy Dick Dale staccato picking tk-tk-tk-tk-tkt on those strings—it sounded like the barrel of a goddamn wave.

This is, clearly, someone who in his life's work identifies very strongly with his passion for surfing. He's talking about the sensation of balancing on your surfboard, being inside the curve of the wave, where you can stretch out a hand and touch the inside of wall of water as you go past. He says in the same interview one other comment about the wateriness of his life that I found quite moving as well: talking about enduring health problems, he explains,

> "Alright, I smoked cigarettes, and then I quit smoking when I couldn't talk properly anymore and my lungs filled up and they sounded like a fucking ocean."

He has the sea around him in his music, he surfs in it frequently, and it also fills up his very lungs and his hearing. He's in it; it's in him.

One of the reasons Dick Dale was famous in the music world, and is often credited as the father of heavy metal, is that he played so loudly. He'd turn the amps up to eleven and burst them even then. Leo Fender, the eponymous owner of the electric guitar company, collaborated with Dale to design ever-more powerful amplifiers. "When it [an amplifier] can withstand the barrage of punishment from Dick Dale, then it is fit for human consumption," said Fender, approvingly.

I like that Dale just glides along the line that separates excessive noise from silence. He's got his rumble, his "weeer" and his "tk-tk-tk-tk," in front of the roaring crowds, he's turning it up and the noise is all around him, then there's the pop of a valve, a fuse bursts, there's a sudden roaring silence all over the stage where the music was meant to be. And Dale's right here at the interface, just keeping control over, this division between extremes, the loud from the no-noise.

It's a crashing between extremes that you notice also in the description of shark attacks on people. Just browsing my shark book library, here's, for example, Sanford Moss in *Sharks: an Introduction for the Amateur Naturalist* (1984). He says:

> Rodney Fox never saw the great white that savaged him off Aldinga Beach in 1963 until he felt the cruel teeth lacerating his flesh. He was conscious only of a sudden stillness in the water around him, '. . . a silence, a perceptible hush'. Diver Henri Bource, too, experienced the same eerie silence of a sea suddenly empty of the seals and fish that moments before he had been photographing.

If it all falls quiet, that is the moment to worry.

Thinking back to Ahab in the water, it was ambiguous as to whether he's the silent protagonist or the astonished victim. Or both, killer and killed, in a bubble of silence. Similarly looking at an issue from both sides, for

CARDIAC RESPONSES TO SOUNDS IN *NEGAPRION* 535

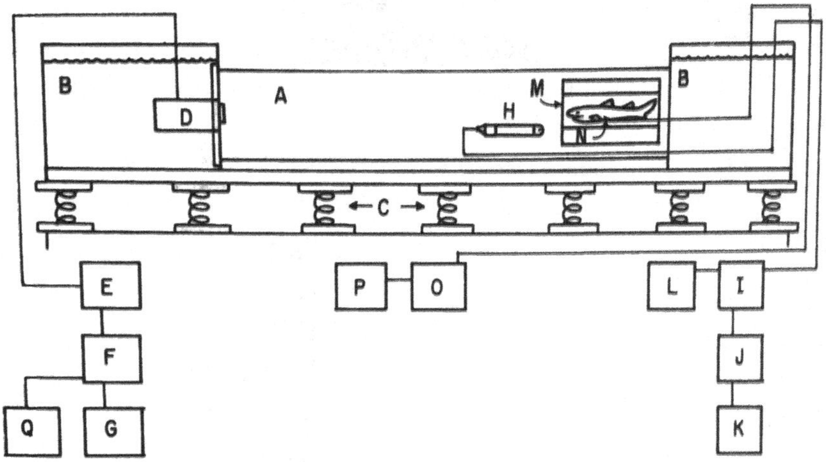

Fig. 35–2 **The sound-tunnel apparatus (diagrammatic) used for the determination of heart-response thresholds. A. PVC plastic pipe (length, 20′: ID, 11″). B. End boxes (plywood). C. Sound damping springs. D. J9 transducer. E. Amplifier. F. Attenuator-photoswitch panel. G. Oscillator. H. Hydrophone. I. Sound-level meter. J. Electronic filter. K. Vacuum-tube voltmeter. L. Oscilloscope. M. Plexiglas restrainer. N. EKG electrode. O. Low-level preamplifier. P. EKG recorder. Q. Random-noise generator.**

Fig. 35-2, "Cardiac Responses to Sounds in Negaprion," Donald R. Nelson in *Sharks, Skates, and Rays*, ed. Perry Gilbert et al., 1967

fairness, I wondered how the shark attack appears to the shark. Everything might, in the preceding moment, go very quiet for the victim, but what does the shark hear?

Back to my shark library, (to Rodney Steel, *Sharks of the World*, of 1985), who explains in detail about the ear of the shark, but who disclaims that "Precisely what sharks can hear is unknown;" apparently they lack the sophisticated cochlear mechanisms that allow for "verbal communication and the composition of music." Sharks can't do this. But they do retain an inner ear system consisting of chambers and canals—it sounds like Venice—chambers and canals lined in places with delicate hairs. These hairs are rooted in cells which register motion, and translate it into electrical signal that are then sent to the brain. Like the stylus on a record player, a thin strand that picks up good vibrations from the vinyl.

At the opposite end from the roots, the hairs in the shark's ear have their top ends stuck into what Steel rather nicely calls "a calcified otolith" which is, "a rather crumbly, amorphous mass of crystals." (From the ancient Greek, *otolith* means "ear-stone.")

Moss, the other shark biologist, in contrast, states that "the shark otolith has the consistency of thick cream." They might both be right, with crystal and cream; sharks differ enormously by species and age. In any case, the otolith shifts about as the shark moves, but with a degree of inertia. So the hairs measure the delay between the movement as it's perceived in the hair follicle, and the slightly lagging movement in the otolith, at the other end of the hair. By registering these small differences, the shark is able to calculate its speed, acceleration, position, balance.

This otolith—on the hair in the chamber in the ear in the shark—is formed of calcium carbonate, a mineral that's found, variously, as far away as Mars; here, in foods like broccoli; geologically, in chalk and limestone. I found this curious, a mineral substance in the heart of the shark's auditory system, which is really its balance and movement (or, surfing) system. It caught my attention because there's another set-up with a chunk of mineral at the centre of the labyrinth, and that's the crystal radio set.

This is, old-fashioned radio, what was used by Marconi and co. until its replacement in the 1920s by the tube receiver (that's vacuum tube, not big wave tube). A crystal radio set contains: an antenna, a resonant circuit, a detector, and an earphone: unlike Dick Dale, it's got no amplifying components. At the centre of the set-up is the demodulator, which is a small blob of crystal and a short length of metal wire.

You set up your radio by adjusting the relative positions of these, finding the fine line to receive your signal not noise. I mentioned earlier how Dale seems to surf the interface between excessive noise and silence, a metaphor of motion. I like how with the radio we have "static," the noise of not moving, just fuzzy.

For these components, the wire in a crystal radio was usually phosphor bronze; the crystal itself was most often made of galena, which is lead sulfide. Now I'll detour into etymology.

Galena is the substance in the radio set. The name derives from the ancient Greek *galene*, which is, "the stillness of the sea; a calm." Its meanings are, first, maritime, and then, metaphorically, referring to mental calm, serenity. It's just through chance (and lexicography) that this *galene* lands in my ears, spirals through my cochlea and washes up in my language field, right next to *galeos*, which is the ancient Greek for "shark." And which gives us *galeus*, which is a genus of shark: the saw-tailed catshark.

I like this adjacency, the way that a galeos or shark, oriented and balanced by the calcified mineral in its ear, this galeos swims, linguistically and functionally, alongside the radio, with the galena at its centre.

It's like the shark is an autonomous, mobile receiver, ploughing around all over the ocean, with its receiving set-up there in the ear, just tuned in to the right frequencies. It's hitting the longitudes, appreciating the waves, or sometimes just the galene, the stillness. And everyone—sharks, radio enthusiasts, us—everyone is listening carefully. Waiting for Dick Dale to start with the thrumming and TKTKTK. Waiting for the silence, the noise, the silence.

I'll go quiet now.

Gold and copper alloy spiral earring with lion-griffin head terminal, Cyprus, first half of the fifth century BC. Met Museum, the Cesnola Collection, purchased by subscription, 1874–76. Public domain

Thomas Walton

Unsavory Thoughts

Fairytale of the Scarecrow

There was an orange man who had no brain. A scarecrow, and we were scared. We were scared because he had no brain, no brain and yet we made him president. We made him president because he had no brain. We are a funny people. We had no brain.

Anyway, we and he had no brain, and he was president. He had no hair, of sorts. The hair was something like straw, but not thick like straw. More like what is on a sow's teats, a hog or pig. He had no hair but only what's on a sow's teats. We called him orange-headed anyway, if we called him at all.

His face, too, was orange. He had no face. He was two-faced, three-faced. It didn't matter. He couldn't see. No eyes on his no-face. No mouth that said anything others didn't say. The mouth just opened and words came out. The words didn't always make sense. Sometimes they weren't even words, just sounds. In this he was very much like us.

The orange man with no brain or face or sense also had no penis, though he had several kids. Each of his kids was a penis in their own right. At least, they were dickheads. He had no spine, the orange man who was president. No stomach for it. No balls or gall. There was nothing to him, really, this scarecrow we made president.

Nothing to him and nothing really left to say. Some thought he was the greatest man who ever lived.

You Can Say Goodbye Now

One day my grandfather stuffed two double cheeseburgers down his throat and died. I know because I was there. I had seven single hamburgers with ketchup and mustard. I was young so I didn't die. I was a teenager. I could eat that much. But my grandfather . . . well, you can't just keep adding cheeseburgers to yourself for seventy years and not expect to one day die.

He didn't die immediately. We went bowling first. He bowled well, generally speaking. With grace, which to me was always more important than the score. I loved watching him bowl. So tall and so living, breathing. Like a dancer or the bass player in a jazz band. He seemed to remove himself and let the bowling ball flow through him. I'll never forget it. I hope I never forget it.

When he took us home (I was too young to drive) he was still alive. And when I waved goodbye, alive. And he drove off alive and I thought nothing of it. I never saw him again. I never saw him alive again.

That night, while we were watching The Cosby Show, he died. He wasn't watching The Cosby Show I don't think, though I guess I don't know what they were watching. Back then, in the 80s, everyone watched something. You sort of had to.

Anyway, we were watching The Cosby Show at our house, and my grandparents were watching something else (I guess) at their condo on the east side. My grandma said he poured two martinis down his throat and died. No one argued with her. We all accepted it. They were of the ratpack generation. Cocktails were part of every evening. I suppose I'm third generation ratpack.

My grandmother called from the hospital. My grandfather was already dead. My father was on the phone with her for what seemed like forever. He even turned off the TV. After some time, we all piled in the station wagon and went to the hospital. I had never been to a hospital before, accept to get my broken arm fixed, but I don't remember it. I think I was in shock.

When we got to the hospital, he was still dead. I thought he wouldn't be, but he was. He still was and he still is. He was always a very stubborn man in that way. My mother said, "would you like to hold his hand?"

I was surprised and didn't know what to do. I was in shock again, I think. I just let her lead me over to him and she grabbed my hand and grabbed my grandfather's hand and put his hand in mine. It was heavy and cold and I held it but was very confused about why I was holding it and what I was supposed to feel. I was scared. And profoundly sad, but the sadness was still in the shock place.

"Would you like to say goodbye?" my mom asked me.

"Okay," I said, but I just stood there, holding the hand and looking at the head that looked like my grandfather's head but clearly wasn't. Clearly was something else now. Something terrible and nothing like the head that I'd seen on top of the elegant body rolling the bowling ball down the lane and sliding ever so slightly across the polished wood floor.

"Go ahead," my mother said, "you can say goodbye now."

All Cops Are Aphorists

I lived on the street for a few years when I was a teenager. It was my right, so I did it. I didn't want to pay rent, or work a job, or go to college, or live with my parents, so I lived on the street. It's easy to move onto the street. You just walk out onto the street and stay there. You don't have to fill out any applications or provide references. There's no credit check. You just go stand around somewhere, or walk around somewhere, and after a while you're living on the street.

If you wanted, you could work for money. You didn't have to, but you could if you wanted. I worked as a harmonica player for a few dollars a day. It was enough for me.

I met some friends in New Orleans who felt the same way I did. They too were living on the street. We began hanging out together. We drank coffee for long hours in the all-night cafes. We busked together. My friend Jason could play any song any tourist requested, and we sang the lyrics when we knew them, and improvised when we didn't. We pooled our money. We had wild parties on Jackson Square. Everyone was invited. All the tourists stared. After the parties we slept in doorways, or on the riverbank, or in St. Claude Cemetery. It was easy to climb over the wall of the cemetery. The cops never bothered us there.

The cops didn't like us. Nobody really liked us. Sometimes tourists took our picture. I'm sure there's several pictures of Jason and I in several closets in several states in the Midwest. Sometimes the cops arrested us. Mostly they told us to move on, no loitering, etc.

We did what they said. We walked around the block and resumed our party somewhere else, until the cops showed up again. When they got sick of this game, especially if there was a big festival coming up—Mardi Gras or JazzFest—they would arrest us and take us to Orleans Parish Prison.

Orleans Parish Prison was not a nice place. It was a cold and violent place. But we all agreed the food there was better than the food at the homeless shelters where we went sometimes to get rice and . . . rice and some undefinable gumbo-like thing in the shape of a blood splat served on a tan plastic tray. We learned very quickly to avoid the soup kitchens and the cops. All my friends hated the cops and would sometimes yell at them and flip them off. I liked the cops. I felt bad for them. Except when they beat us up. I didn't like that, but even that was a kind of truth. There was a lot of truth in the things they did and said:

"You just can't stay here" "You have to leave" "No loitering" etc.

These were aphorisms as true as those of the ancient prophets. And now look at me. No longer there. No longer young. No longer working as a harmonica player. I did have to move on. And Jason, too. He drank himself to death ten years ago. Or rather, he died ten years ago after drinking himself to death day after day, year after year. He drank and drank from the time we were teenagers living on the street and singing "Gin and Juice" and "The Old Laughing Lady." In New Orleans and Louisville, San Francisco, Seattle, Santa Fe, and several dozen towns and cities in between.

Jason's gone now. The cops were assholes. They were brutal at times, but they spoke the truth. You just can't stay here. You have to leave.

IM NOT LIVING
IM JUST KILLING TIME

ALOE VERA
BIBLE VERSES
CLEAN EATING
DETOX
ESSENTIAL OILS
FLAX SEED
GARLIC
HEALING CRYSTALS
INSPIRATIONAL QUOTES
PETROLEUM JELLY
KOMBUCHA
LEMON JUICE
MOON LIGHT
NATURE
ORGANIC EGGS
POSITIVE THINKING
QUAKERISM
RUBBING ACTIVATED CHARCOAL
SNAKE VENOM
TREE BARK
URINE
VITAMIN WATER
WEIGHT LOSS PILLS
YAK'S MILK
ZEN OUT

Marvin Cohen

Almost an Interview with W.H. Auden

Mr Auden's familiar craggy-flabby face was labryinthinely lined with webs and mats of wrinkled flesh. He wore a frayed tweed-plaid jacket with a pipe stem sticking up from the chest pocket. His shoes and pants were strictly for comfort, and durability. He was slightly high on drink, and his disposition was professional-amiable: he owed a friendly duty to the public to occasionally submit to interviews when trapped in London. Location: penthouse garden atop Arts Council building on Piccadilly overlooking Green Park, London, 1970.

COHEN: Why are you in London?

AUDEN: For the poetry festival. *(He was to read from his poetry at Queen Elizabeth Hall the following night.)*

COHEN: Where do you spend your year?

AUDEN: Five months in New York, five months in Austria, and about one month in England.

COHEN: What do you do when you're in England?

AUDEN: My friends and family are here. I see them.

COHEN: Then why don't you live here longer instead of just visit?

AUDEN: I adore my family, but I don't want to live with them.

COHEN: Why do you prefer New York to London?

AUDEN: London is too provincial.

COHEN: I'm surprised to hear you say that. Can you elaborate?

AUDEN: New York is the only city I know that's not provincial.

COHEN: But how is London provincial? What do you mean by provincial?

AUDEN: Don't trap me into semantics. Beginning with 'insularity,' do you want a declension and derivation fest?

COHEN: What do you think of the state of England today?

AUDEN: England has become the center of vulgarity.

COHEN: But surely isn't the United States more vulgar?

AUDEN: The United States is nowhere close. No other country in the world compares with England's vulgarity. There's nothing to compare with going up and down the tube escalator and seeing such unadulteratedly vulgar ads. The obscenity isn't even explained, it just hits you in the eye, it's there before you. New York advertisers wouldn't dare be so blatant.

COHEN: In what other way is England vulgar?

AUDEN: Those brash little miniskirts. There's no attempt to justify them by aesthetic proportion in fashioning. The dresses aren't made to be beautiful, but to reveal barely. The celebrated old Roman decadence may have had time to become more notorious than ours—but it didn't exceed ours.

COHEN: You're down on England?

AUDEN: I'm down on aspects of today's England—aspects which, unchecked, have been allowed to grow dominant. The vulgarity of magazines, both the Sundays and the glossies. The loud, impossible noises of fad music. Shallowness made into a goddess, the surface into a cult. The fashion mania. The tastelessness, the senselessness, which alas has become so prevalent in England. I just don't belong to it—I can't.

COHEN: What of today's youth?

AUDEN: I feel sorry for them. I pity them.

COHEN: How do you mean?

AUDEN: When I was young, I was never bored. No one was, then. One always was interested in something—in cricket, in nature, in books, in travel. Today, the young do seem bored. And rootless. They're not connected with the past. And not being connected with the past, they seem terribly devoid of a future. They have no confidence in what, if anything, is to come. That's why they act out of desperation, for the immediate. They stamp right out into violence, into sensation. There's such a vacuum, they've got to fill it –loudly, pleasurably, for its own sake, hedonistically; they act not out of what will be, or from what was, but into an aimless and desperate pleasure that dies out quickly and bears no fruit. These wild fits are sterile. I can only pity the young who are like that.

COHEN: But why must living necessarily relate to the past? Can't it have its own spontaneous reason for being?

AUDEN: You can't lead a human life without communication with the dead.

COHEN: That's a memorable statement. And what do you think of man's imminence on the moon?

AUDEN: A load of balls. What does it all matter, this space exploration, and just what does it prove? Man can't exceed his own measure, which is himself. Going to the moon has no philosophical or theological value. Man must be concerned with understanding things close to home, and no outward planet can furnish a clue to the problems immemorial to man's soul.

COHEN: You're essentially a conservatist?

AUDEN: But I'm really freer than those uniformed "rebels" you see all over today, those hippies or beatniks all uniformed in their conformity of revolt, in their mindless, directionless rebellion. They're as much uniformed as their accountant and barrister fathers.

COHEN: They're in despair, and there's no solution?

AUDEN: Their despair is more apathy. I don't know of a solution.

COHEN: When you were young, weren't you dissatisfied?

AUDEN: When I was young, I lacked for nothing. I accepted my parents' values implicitly. Not that there wasn't an occasional point or fact that I didn't dispute. But in general, I didn't question their values. I had everything I needed.

COHEN: Your family was well off?

AUDEN: No, they weren't, and I don't mean it that way. They had to work hard, but they sacrificed for me, and I had every advantage. I had everything I wanted, and needed: a very good education, enough books, enough leisure, good friends, the opportunity to travel. I was given warmth and love by my family. I didn't feel misplaced. All my interests followed from a secure root. My numerous diversifications as I grew older and acquired more interests were all the branchings out from something well based.

COHEN: You have so much to be grateful for—

AUDEN:—And not the least of my good fortune was a solid classical education. I was steeped in Greek and Latin. It taught me to use words carefully, with the exact shade of meaning, when I came to write poetry. They were invaluable, irreplaceable lessons for what was to become my profession of letters.

COHEN: Language today is abused?

AUDEN: Horribly. The young rebels often use language so loosely and inadequately that I can sense the disrespect they have for it. And not they only, but politicians as well. It's alarming. I recently heard a politician, in praising a colleague, use the phrase "integrity-ridden!"

COHEN: And he meant it favorably?

AUDEN: Yes! Can you believe it?

COHEN: Can you make a living by your poetry?

AUDEN: No, no one can. The occasional stray novelist can—usually if he's bad. Poetry earns me dribs and drabs, but the bulk of my living is through other writing, and editing.

COHEN: Are you writing a lot of poetry now?

AUDEN: Yes, I think so.

COHEN: Do you like it?

AUDEN: I have to, otherwise I wouldn't be writing it. A poet doesn't write for money, he writes for joy.

COHEN: Do you alter your styles from time to time?

AUDEN: I must. When a writer finds himself having gotten into the habit of a verbal technique, he must break it—or he rapidly becomes sterile in it. He must make fresh use of language, if it's to lead him to strange delight—which, after all, is the "purpose" of it all.

COHEN: You thoroughly studied Greek and Latin, that's known. But did you ever take any courses in creative writing?

AUDEN: That would have been balls! It's impossible to teach "creative writing." And it can be harmful, it can mislead.

COHEN: How do you feel about Vietnam?

AUDEN: Let's not discuss it, please.

COHEN: You find the world immeasurably changed?

AUDEN: I cling to what I've known and accepted, though I must remain realistic about what's happening now. If there are names in poems, poets have to explain them now. Any mythological or classical reference, there's probably got to be a footnote for: today's reader can't be trusted to know the references. Our backgrounds and education and reading are so varied, that it's hit or miss, very chancy, whether one person has read the same book as another. In Homer's day, Homer could afford to use a lot of proper names in his epics, he was able to assume that all his readers were familiar with them. That was an ideal advantage for a poet to have. But through the ages it's become less and less like that, though never so drastically impossible as today's situation. We must have communication with the past, with the dead. Otherwise our mental life-line is broken.

The above was published in [Arts in Society, vol 12/3, 1975] with the title: An Interview with W.H.Auden. However, Marvin Cohen later confessed it was "a literary hoax and that all of W.H.'s lines were sheer Marvinisms." [W.H. Auden Society Newsletter, 2002].

A recent email exchange (September, 2022) between Marvin and Colin Myers (then unaware of Marvin's prior confession) confirms this:

CM: On a completely different note: some time ago I read your interview with W.H.Auden. I wonder what he was like to interview (or as a person or poet).

MC: My interview with him was an invented phony. I was hungry for some kind of recognition, so I was brazen with name-dropping arrogance. The introduction was from my friend Gerard Hughes, who was Ted's brother. *(in a later conversation, Marvin said it was actually Ted's sister Olwyn).* I don't remember any exchanged words between me and Auden, or even if he had any wrinkles on his face. We remained anonymous to each other.

CM: Did you actually do an interview? Are they his actual words and your actual words? I am intrigued.

MC: I don't remember any actual words either by me or him; maybe there were none. I was an opportunistic desperate hustler, a chancer, with no moral integrity.

CM: Did you actually see him? Or was the entire interview a fabrication?

MC: I asked my eyes if they saw him, and they remembered yes, but then they remembered no. But then they said I Auden'd to ask such questions.

CM: Did Auden ever find out?

MC: I don't know if he ever found out. I imagine he lacked the vanity to care.

Note: Marvin very much likes Auden's poetry.

Kurt Luchs

From One American Original to Another: Lucille Clifton On Crazy Horse

If I ever manage to finish my first novel, some people are bound to ask, "Which parts are real, and which are fiction?" The answer will be, "It's all fiction, and it's all real." Meaning: I'm making it up, even the parts seemingly drawn from my own life, and if I do my job well, the story will reveal some novel (no pun intended) aspects of our shared reality, something new under the sun that only my imagination and life experience could bring about. Anyway, don't hold your breath.

"To know thyself is the beginning of wisdom," said Socrates; and, he might have added, the beginning of the writer's journey as well. But not the end. The whole point of the writer's awareness is surely to enter imaginatively into the hearts and minds of other characters and things, people, animals, plants, the world itself. This imagining usually starts with the first tool of human understanding, also the first tool in the poet's toolbox: analogy, or simile, likeness or its opposite, unlikeness.

Which brings us to Lucille Clifton (1936-2010). Being born a Black woman in America, and coming of age just as the civil rights movement was taking off, she wrote frequently and movingly about those experiences. A little younger than Maya Angelou (born 1928) and a little older than Nikki Giovanni (born 1943), she has much in common with those two contemporaries and other African American writers. What sets her apart from them and from almost any other poets of her generation is her unique combination of gifts, particularly her gift for empathy and her gift for concision. The former is what enables her to inhabit the spirit of Crazy Horse; the latter is largely responsible for making the result so memorable.

Clifton wrote five poems about the Lakota Oglala Sioux war chief who orchestrated the defeat of General Custer at the Battle of Little Bighorn in 1876. The poems "the death of crazy horse," "crazy horse names his daughter," "crazy horse instructs the young men but in their grief they forget," and "the message of crazy horse" all appear in the volume *Next* (1987). The fifth poem, "witko," appears in the final book of poetry Clifton published during her lifetime, *Voices* (2008).

We are looking today at "the message of crazy horse," the last of the four poems about him in *Next*. It serves as a comment on his life and the state of the world, made all these years later by his own spirit, as pictured by Clifton. The poem contains 18 lines of free verse broken into five stanzas, the first three consisting of three lines each, the fourth of four lines and the fifth of five lines, a breakdown that suggests a homemade kind of form. One reason the poem works as well as it does is that Clifton's concise language matches the laconic nature of Native oratory. You feel that if she and Crazy Horse had ever met, each would have understood the other's refusal to waste words.

The first three stanzas, the shorter ones, recount the emotional and spiritual highlights of his life—which, significantly, do not include his battle triumphs. I take this pointed omission of the events for which he is most famous as a reminder that the necessities and duties of war were thrust upon him, not something he wished for or welcomed. In this, ironically, he has much more in common with an earlier American warrior, George Washington, than with his contemporary and opponent George Custer.

In the dramatic monologue that Clifton has crafted for him, the spirit of Crazy Horse begins at the beginning:

> i would sit in the center of the world,
> the Black Hills hooped around me and
> dream of my dancing horse [. . .]

Almost all people feel a special love for their homeland, and may also feel, or even believe, that it's the center of the world. The Lakota and other members of the Oglala Sioux band believed the Black Hills to be the literal center of the world—not just of their world—and anyone who has visited there might be tempted to agree with them. To paraphrase a line from later in the poem, their medicine is strong. So it is appropriate that "the message of crazy horse" mentions his Black Hills homeland first. What might seem odd is that he mentions his horse before his wife, daughter and lover. What's that about? I think it's because he was famed as a horseman and "horse" became part of his name before he fell in love, took a wife and fathered a child. He's simply telling his story chronologically. It may also be an oblique way of getting his war deeds into the poem after all, seeing as his skills as a rider were crucial to his war victories.

All he says in the poem about the woman Black Shawl is that she was his wife and bore him the daughter he named They Are Afraid of Her, though no one ever got the chance to be afraid of her as she died at age three. (There was a second wife later, Nellie Larrabee, daughter of a French trader and a Cheyenne woman, but she informed on Crazy Horse for the U.S. military, so the sincerity of that marriage is doubtful.) The poem starts to take off at the juncture between the end of stanza two and the beginning of stanza three:

> i was afraid of nothing
>
> except Black Buffalo Woman.
> my love for her i wore
> instead of feathers. [. . .]

Black Buffalo Woman was the love of his life. There were difficulties; they never married. Instead she wed a brave named No Water. However, the love between her and Crazy Horse continued to smolder, and one day they ran off together. When No Water caught up with them he shot Crazy Horse in the face with a pistol, leaving a permanent scar in the shape of a lightning bolt, which fit another part of the prophecy from his vision quest. You can't make this stuff up!

The line about not wearing feathers is another reference to Crazy Horse's life-changing vision, in which he was instructed not to wear war paint or a traditional feather headdress into battle. As long as he dressed modestly and didn't take scalps or other war trophies, he would be victorious and could not be killed in battle. For the most part, these prophecies proved to be true. The only time he was seriously wounded in combat was when he broke his vow by taking a scalp. More than a year after the Battle of Little Bighorn, when it was clear his cause was lost, Crazy Horse surrendered to the U.S. authorities and on September 5, 1877, wound up at Fort Robinson, Nebraska. That night he was bayoneted by a guard, supposedly while trying to escape, and died hours later. His parents collected the remains the next morning and laid him to rest in a location that remains secret to this day.

Back to the poem. This is about a poem, remember? After the three opening stanzas recounting highlights of Crazy Horse's time on earth, the narrative slips into high gear:

> [. . .] i did not dance
>
> i dreamed. i am dreaming now
> across the worlds. my medicine is strong.
> my medicine is strong in the Black basket
> of these fingers. [. . .]

The last words of stanza three refer again to his vision quest, which told him he was not to engage in the usual war dances. As reimagined by Clifton, his mission both before and after death was dreaming. One of the author's chief poetic devices, just as it is one of the chief rhetorical devices of Native oratory, is reiteration. It's been sneaking up on us in stanzas one through three in the use of the word "Black"—capitalized because in each instance it is part of a proper name—and in the word "afraid"—first as part of his daughter's name, and then to describe the one thing he is afraid of, Black Buffalo Woman, thus neatly tying up the two reiterated words together.

The use of reiteration reaches its peak in stanza four, which can be considered the hinge of the poem, the place where it turns. "i dreamed", Crazy Horse says, and coming right after the life highlights of stanzas one through three, this tells us that his dream, his vision, was the key to his life. "i am dreaming now across the worlds", he continues, which tells us that his dream is also the key to his afterlife. Then comes the only reiteration of a complete phrase in the poem: "my medicine is strong. / my medicine is strong in the Black basket / of these fingers." Well, his medicine would have to be strong for his spirit to still be out there somewhere with something important to convey to us. And what an evocative, mysterious image that is, "the Black basket / of these fingers." I understand it as a reference to his physical death and the way the fingers of the Black Hills continue to hold his remains in an undisclosed location. Is that the reason "Black" is once again capitalized? Or is this the place where the author asserts her own personal identification with Crazy Horse, her Blackness linking her to this notable member of another oppressed and dispossessed group? Both, I think. And as Bob Dylan says somewhere (I believe in an early Playboy interview), "Mystery is a traditional fact."

Another mystery is the second mention of Black Buffalo Woman that begins the final stanza, number five. Special emphasis is being given to her, because her name is the only one mentioned twice in the poem, underscoring her centrality to the speaker. The most mysterious thing about it, to me, is that Clifton chooses not to capitalize the "w" in "woman" this time. I have no idea what this means though it is clearly deliberate. The only other name in which the initial letters are not capitalized is that of Crazy Horse himself, in both the title of the poem and the last line (and also in the use of a lower-case "i" when he speaks in the first person). This is not mysterious. Rather, it reflects the man's essential humility, something he shares with the author who uses a lower-case "i" in her other poems after the manner of e. e. cummings.

After invoking Black Buffalo Woman's name again and asking her to hear him, Crazy Horse delivers his new vision, and unlike his original vision quest it is not a happy or hopeful one:

> the hoop of the world is breaking.
> fire burns in the four directions.

the dreamers are running away from the hills.
i have seen it. i am crazy horse.

Only here, in the climax to this remarkable poem, does it become plain that we are reading an apocalyptic vision. The line "the hoop of the world is breaking" reminds us of a similar line near the beginning of the vision vouchsafed to W. B. Yeats in "The Second Coming": "Things fall apart; the centre cannot hold". Knowing that Clifton was quite familiar with the King James Bible, I also hear an echo of the apocalypse from Revelation 1: 18: "I am he that liveth, and was dead; and behold, I am alive for evermore, Amen, and have the keys of hell and of death." This sounds very like her Crazy Horse, yes? And the fire burning in the next line resonates with those of us raised in a Christian culture to fear Hell.

Yet the worst news is saved for the penultimate line, "the dreamers are running away from the hills". It was bad enough that the U.S. government forcibly removed the Natives from their homes and homeland. This line brings us right up to the present, in which the dreamers, the visionaries, have fled from what gives them visions without being forced. To quote the Bible a final time, "Where there is no vision, the people perish" (Proverbs 29:18). With this line, I believe, the poem comes full circle, making its own hoop. The identification of author Lucille Clifton with the speaker of her dramatic monologue, Crazy Horse, becomes complete. She too is a visionary. Without the visions of dreamers like her and Crazy Horse, the people indeed perish, and perhaps also the earth on which they walk.

The last line—"i have seen it. i am crazy horse."—serves as a signature and a bona fide. This is the same Crazy Horse whose original vision proved to be true. We can trust him on this one. And the power of the vision comes as much from understatement as anything, the understatement common to Native oratory and Clifton's brilliant poetics.

Kurt Luchs

Near Death

Flying into Phoenix on a Friday morning
we hit a wind shear so sharp
it knocked us sideways and down,
dropping 5,000 feet in a minute and a half,
the longest 90 seconds of our lives.
Every person on that plane
knew they were about to perish in it.
Suddenly weightless, we levitated out of our seats
and headfirst into the cabin ceiling,
meals and drinks sailing, luggage bursting
from the overhead bins into skulls and bodies
already reeling. Even the flight attendants

were screaming, and the young woman next to me
dug her nails into my arm and shrieked,
"We're crashing! We're crashing!"
Ever the gentleman, and always helpful in a crisis,
I reminded her of what Crazy Horse said
right before the Battle of the Little Big Horn:
"Today is a good day to die."
"What the fuck are you talking about?"
she yelled, but it worked—for a few
crucial seconds she was distracted from her fear.
I was afraid too, of course, though oddly
not for my life or death,
and after we had landed safely, I realized why.
Being hit and run and left for dead
by a semi-truck driver some years ago
had made me painfully aware that I was not
ready for death, that my soul
and psyche were in terrible shape.
Since then I had slain what inner demons I could
and put the rest in chains. At last I was living
as authentically as I knew how.
I had done the most terrifying thing imaginable—
become a father. I had even dared to start writing.
I had everything to live for and no wish to die.
This everyday American mongrel,
part Norwegian, part Irish, part German Jew,
2.6 percent Neanderthal
and one sixty-fourth Shawnee
from the mighty war chief Corn Stalk,
this mostly white man is not worthy
to share the same sentence with Crazy Horse.
Yet by virtue of our common humanity
I claimed and still claim the right
to find inspiration in his final recorded words:
"Today is a good day to die."
And also to live, great spirit,
and also to live.

The Butterfly Cemetery
Franca Mancinelli (trans. John Taylor)
The Bitter Oleander Press, April 2022

Award winning poet Franca Mancinelli's *The Butterfly Cemetery*, translated into English by John Taylor, collects thirteen years of prose writings including fiction, autobiography, and essays on writing. "Poetry, Mother Tongue" points toward one node of its connections, in its evocation of an interdependent relationship between one's inner reader and writer: "More than in dreaming, the origin of poetry seems to lie on this threshold between sleeping and wakefulness, in which we are given back to ourselves, naked, entirely and now only a gaze, entirely and only listening" (133). In a formal mirroring of these assertions, a common feature throughout this varied collection is the presence of open, unspoken space that allows—in fact, requires—the reader to think through correlations and implications and attend to emotional and psychological resonances, often by immersing themselves both cognitively and emotionally in the experiences of images and scenes. Although there is much more to explore in the collection within themes including childhood, psychological healing, and landscape, I will look closely at several pieces that reflect an overarching interest in various forms of such deep reading, broadly understood.

The short fiction "The Little Girl Who Learned How to Fly" opens with a gesture connecting reading and observation as the girl watches a bird through her window: "The rustling and the small beating sounds it made seemed letters of an alphabet to be deciphered." Next, she follows it outside: "She looked back into the biggest puddle: there it was, resting on something invisible. She couldn't help but touch it with her finger, slowly, so that it wouldn't fly away. But as soon as her finger broke the surface of the water, the bird vanished." The puddle replaces the window as the lens of viewing the image, a movement that indicates dually an entry into the bird's own world yet a literal rather than reflected understanding of the image. Finally, while "thinking about where it might be," the girl transforms into a bird in vivid Ovidian description. In her new form, "She stopped to look down at the garden, the house where she had lived, and headed straight for the blue" (33).

How quickly and seamlessly we have moved from the discovery of the bird whose "text" we needed to learn to read on its own terms, to the illusion of concrete understanding, to full imaginative immersion that transports us not only outside of our home but also outside of the laws of the physical world, to view it from the reflective distance of the imagined perspective we have inhabited. Importantly, the girl's "thinking" and imagining the bird collaborate in this movement. Given this underlying psychological progression, the story can read as an engaging allegory in which the recursive and reflective reader may perceive themselves in the act of imaginative reading, creating within the psyche a mirror of the text which gives way to a fully imagined one, from which we can see our own world "from the outside" within us. However, inextricable from the moorings of these thoughts are the *sensations* of the child's curiosity, the transformation, the heading "for blue," the exhilaration of imaginative reading and its intrinsic experience of selfhood as the interior exploration of the other. We want to learn from reading, of course, but first the reading must make us want to read.

An autobiographical piece, "Inside a Horizon of Hills," recalls another sequence of readings, in this case of childhood landscapes:

> It did not allow itself to be embraced by reason; it kept eluding me like things traversed by the shock of beauty, like the greatest loves. The object of love is known by reducing it to more understandable and controllable parts; the ruinous flood of passion is held in check by channeling it towards fragments, details. This is why I often isolated trees from that line of hills.... (81)

Here, Mancinelli provides a more objective description of the complementary processes of interpretation and imagination of alterity, located for her childhood self in "this unmarked limit between the plain and the hills" where her "imagination gravitated around this point where two worlds joined" (83). She weaves these memories with the region's history and literary embodiments in Pavese, whose narratives she credits with offering her the imaginative approach of reading the objects of the landscape thereafter. The ending, from a memory of exploring nighttime fields alone as an adolescent, shows another view of the genuine and palpable surprises that are possible when imaginative reading relocates us, in this case quite literally, *within* the "text":

> Only the land was tilting, losing all boundaries, entering more and more into the night. A land so dark and devastated that my eyes had to follow every footstep: every moment seemed to surge forth beneath my feet, emerge and withdraw. I was at the beginning of the world. A strange grace kept my hands raised and open, like a scarecrow lingering in the now deserted field. A few minutes of pure emptiness went by. Then I was surprised by the howl of a dog. (85)

In comparison to the bird in the story, the other here is the more macrocosmic, and the mode is memory refracted through lyrical association rather than fictional narration, yet the manner in which reading the external presence informs ongoing experience and perception of the self is complimentary to the first piece, as is the relational sense of excitement and discovery the process itself is imbued with.

Furthering this diversity of reading experiences, "Living in the Ideal City: Fragments in the Form of Vision" is an interactive ekphrasis made up of "fragments in the form of a vision...born from long immersions in the lake of the *Ideal City*" written by "going and coming back across the threshold of this space that appears and disappears. A space transported and transmuted by thoughts like clouds by the wind" (97). Mancinelli roots the processes of imaginal reading in their interdependent psychological and epistemological contexts: "in this space everything blurs: a daydream within reality, reality within a daydream. Two opposing forces collide: the geometric control and something irreducible to this planned harmony" (95). This work explores another mode of reading in which imaginings and the images that give rise to them alternate roles in the writing like a flexible figure and ground. Working with the images created of another artist's consciousness presents another experience of the permeable membranes between self and other, conscious and unconscious, and creative work's provisional presentations of—and open space for—these complexities.

The third section, grouping various experiential and metaphorical views on writing, also includes insights into the role of reading in authorial development and practice, refreshingly, in ways that bypass the vague stoicism or pseudo morality with which reading is often enjoined to young writers. Rather, Mancinelli offers interesting parables that must themselves be read through thought to reach the reader-writer. In "A Line Is a Lap and Other Notes on Poetry" she details the way a waiter reads tables to "ensure that nobody asks for him" and works in cohort, reading eye contact and nods, to maximize the productivity of each member's movements, concluding: "It sufficed to understand in what way one should write. Or else we will bring books that remain closed, like bottles of water on a table for which only one bottle was needed" (113). The image is at once a pragmatic counsel and a transformative invitation: The books will "remain closed" both in that, practically, reader-writers need to open them to be read, but also because, if reader-writers do not open books, their own books will never "open" themselves with perceptive, engaging, and nuanced work—and then who would want to read them? The teaching challenges the writer to become a deep enough reader to learn from it, evidencing the interconnectedness of the processes in its very mode of communication.

This book isn't a light read, but certainly a bottle worth opening for readers and, of course, writers and artists, who are deeply aware of and concerned with the practices and implications their imaginative work holds for the psyche, our natural and cultural environments, and, perhaps most mysteriously, their own "reader" with many faces.

Vi Khi Nao's *Suicide*: A Meditation on Life

Suicide: The Autoimmune Disorder of the Psyche
Vi Khi Nao
11:11 Press, March 2023

> "There are two types of people in the world: the one who thinks about sex and the one who thinks about death."

This could be a difficult book for many people to read. The title probably gives that away. But this book is not challenging in the ways that most would imagine. *Suicide* was difficult for me as someone who has an intimate relationship with potentially fatal diseases and a fallible body. It is through the body, the living body, that we understand agency and its limits. As Nao chronicles her own health issues, the reader sees that this book is much more about hardships in life than it is about self-murder. Nao's honest examination of intensely personal moments brings to the light how economic, social, and physical factors influence an individual's perception of their own mortality. At its heart, *Suicide* is about the right to control all aspects of your life, including its end.

For those familiar with Nao's oeuvre, this book is different in style from Nao's more experimental works. It is memoir and contains a much more traditional voice than many fans might associate with her. The reader still gets pieces of Nao staples, like food imagery and unique pop-culture metaphors that range from movies to dog breeds to football. The voice in *Suicide*, though, through its stripped-down vignettes and simpler (though not simple) phrasing, gives this work an immediacy and an intimacy. It is incredibly personal and honest.

Suicide opens philosophically, with a litany of famous suicides as Nao deconstructs its taboo. Nao's own relationship with suicidal ideation becomes inextricably linked to several factors in her life, the first and most prominent being health issues related to her heart. Depression and heart disease go hand-in-hand and people who undergo major heart surgeries often suffer from major depressive episodes in their recovery.

"My heart and its murmuring had always made me painfully aware of my existence—the surgery would severely heighten this awareness. I was terrified of living longer. I was so exhausted from being in pain all the time."

Nao mentions, several times, that she wants the pain to stop but it is unclear what type of pain she is referencing because, with illness, there is both physical suffering and its mental toll. Throughout this work, we see how different factors (poverty, disease, heartache, abuse) lead to the contemplation of suicide. A catch-22 exists in that those suffering also experience the pain of "guilt to have to exist". Many people carry on because of this guilt and that, in itself, is a form of stress—an ouroboros of agony. Ultimately, Nao questions free will. Of all of the permissions we need to secure in life, do we really need permission to choose to die? Why does that decision exist outside of the self? Our relationship with death and our own mortality, with the specter of suicide, is at once intensely personal but also somehow shared with everyone we love.

While Nao declares "[i]t's very simple: I am pro-suicide because I am anti-pain," this work is littered with doubt. She questions her decisions, she oscillates in her position on the topic. As she approaches a major surgery, she states: "I had wanted to die for so long and now was the opportunity, but I was conflicted." At one point, the readers sees a typewriter that "seems to posses the ability to erase [her] belief in suicide." Like when her mother says "life is debt," Nao explores the impact of race, finances, and familial obligation on her will to live. To whom do we owe our life? How is it valued? Why shouldn't a person be able to decide when and where their own all ends?

Indecision is the point. Life isn't in binary. Nao is, at once, very much pro-suicide and still conflicted with its presence in her life. The book opens with a giant pi and each section starts with one of its numerals. Life and death are at once part of the same entity and its opposites. *Suicide* is constant and irrational and Nao wraps together the idea of death and life into an infinity. An objective mathematical description of death is perfectly represented when Nao asks, "[i]sn't death ever so remote despite being so near?" In the end, she resolves, as much as she can in an eternal imbalance, that we live for our own reasons and those reasons are personal, though they are inextricable from our identity and relationships. This book does not glorify or condemn suicide; rather, it is a brutally honest exploration of a person's relationship to their own mortality. In her utterly original and exceptional way, Nao interrogates death to show us that what motivates us to live, or not, is intensely personal and still somehow universal.

> "Each time I caress my scar, I understand. If I didn't have this scar I would not be here."

Where Are the Snows
Kathleen Rooney
September 2022, Texas Review Press

Anyone who reads literary journals encounters plenty of po-faced poetry that equates earnestness with seriousness. Don't laugh too much: it might spoil your cred. Humor is a privilege and you'd better check it.

Kathleen Rooney's *Where Are the Snows*, winner of the X.J. Kennedy Prize, evinces a different sensibility. The title refers to François Villon's refrain "Où sont les neiges d'antan?" In the francophone world, this expression has entered everyday speech, with the snows of yesteryear symbolizing an irrecoverable loss. And indeed, Rooney's collection is imbued with a sense of loss, as well as anxiety about the future. At one point, the speaker observes, "This year I gave up hope for Lent."

But note the pith of that line, the resolute weirdness. Only the dourest reader will fail to detect a note of humor amid the bleakness. The first poem in the collection, "Dress Up," introduces a pair of Groucho glasses attached to a big nose and moustache—the "beaglepuss"—and serves as a warning for much of what follows.

> I never forget a face, but in your case I'll be glad to make an exception: us to the 21st century so far.

The beaglepuss is a mask. A mask doesn't only conceal; it can also enable expression. It can allow an individual to speak for herself or even for a community—an "us"—as Paul Laurence Dunbar reminded Americans more than a century ago. Here, a funny mask doesn't preclude engagement with serious issues of our era.

Rooney's quarrel with the 21st century, particularly in regard to the contemporary American scene, emerges gradually over the course of 40 poems, with observations about Maga culture, Covid frustration and economics. In "The Production and Consumption of Goods and Services," the speaker observes

> Why should I die for the economy when he would never do the same for me?
>
> '*Please respect others and only take what you need:* the rule on complimentary tampons and pads in the bathrooms is basically my plan for the entire economy. ...
>
> Freeze and put your hand where I can see it! (I said that to the invisible hand of the market.)

Formally speaking, Rooney relies on free verse stanzas, the best of which possess a well-tuned syntactic snap. There is occasional internal rhyme: "When I can't visit nature, nature visits me: the fattest sparrow on the bare ash tree." She also has a fine eye for image: "Babies in strollers wrapped tight as burritos." Or: "Sick buildings barf their bricky entrails."

This is poetry that wears its quirk on its sleeve, with free-wheeling associative leaps reminiscent of Gregory Corso's much-anthologized "Marriage." Rooney explores the strangeness of literalism ("Why do the woods have a neck anyway?") and the surreal potential of simile ("A dozen oaths, like a box of spiritual donuts").

Many poems rely on the premise of the speaker riffing on one word. "To Cherish a Desire with Anticipation" offers 16 stanzas about *hope*; "Atmospheric Water Vapor Frozen into Ice Crystals" gives us 17 stanzas about *snow*. A poem called "Foretelling the Future by a Randomly Chosen Passage from a Book" appears to be, literally, an aleatory exercise.

The constraints here are less Oulipian than idiosyncratic. Reading some of these poems, I'm reminded of the BBC radio show

"Just a Minute" where a panel of witty guests competes in speaking for one minute about a random topic. The result is entertaining and, in a similar fashion, Rooney seems ready to tackle any subject.

But not all the riffs land home. Some of the poems feel like essays where loosely-associated stanzas replace paragraphs. In "The Surroundings in which an Animal or Plant Lives or Operates," the speaker muses on the anniversary of Earth Day, the BP Deepwater Horizon oil spill, Saint Jerome, Marco Polo, John Berger and Bernard-Henri Lévy. This is only a partial list, and the cumulative effect is not of greater power or resonance but rather dilution.

The best poems in *Where Are the Snows* are more personal, where the speaker acknowledges uncertainty and vulnerability. This uncertainty often refers to an earlier period of religious belief. In "A Talisman Attracts, an Amulet Repels," the speaker asserts

> I long to make a pledge to a saint or a way of life. I long to complete a rite. Would sackcloth and fasting put anything right?
>
> I haven't got faith but I've got an aesthetic.

Or, in "One Authorized to Perform the Sacred Rites"

> My faith remains gone. And yet my ears
> strain. A longing to hear someone in the
> beyond explaining: *Follow the sound of my voice.*

Similar allusions occur throughout the collection. "Like Christ," the speaker says, "we show our wounds reluctantly to doubters." Behind Rooney's humor and political assertions in *Where Are the Snows*, there is longing and sometimes pain of a mind bereft of belief but not of the desire to believe. This convergence of worldly worries and immaterial yearning is perhaps the signature quality of this book, where Rooney the artist succeeds best.

Maes, Angstman, Chasek

Newborn
Agustín Maes
Whiskey Tit, 2020

This excellent novella begins with a jolt: two boys find the abandoned corpse of an infant in a creek. What follows is a wide-ranging exploration of character, place and even time itself. Using multiple points of view, from bewildered participants to an omniscient narrator, *Newborn* tells a big story in a small space.

Set mainly in 1980, it centers on a teenager called Bitsy. She's the mother of the child, a heartbreaking mix of naïve, plucky and tragic. Other characters—the child's father, Art; Donny and Aaron, the boys who find the corpse; and various minor players—are also rendered with precision, and their ignorance of Bitsy's plight in their midst adds layers of complexity.

Maes takes a bold stroke in juxtaposing these human events with descriptions of larger changes in the local reservoir and creek related to the passage of time. Regarding the creek, the omniscient narrator remarks: "By that gentle sound it tells of its beauty and terribleness, its ceaselessness, of how it is inhabited by forms whose forms are fashioned from that habitation."

Nature in this larger sense has its own rhythms, indifferent to human woes and the perplexities of human nature. The omniscient narrator makes proleptic allusions to what characters didn't or couldn't know. In less able hands, this could come off as tricksy or portentous. Or worse, minimizing human pain since hey, we amount to nothing in the Big Picture.

But Maes is more subtle, and the characters' situation gains poignancy for the very fact that it is so ephemeral and much of the suffering is perhaps avoidable. His prose sometimes uses biblical cadences, or suggests the anagogical:

> The child began to move: slow and sluggish, its tiny blue fists quaking uselessly at its sides, stick legs pedaling feebly at the air as though in a leaden jog through the landscape of some dream or nightmare.
> The girl released her breath. "Oh my God."

There are echoes of Cormac McCarthy here, but Maes allows his characters more interiority and, to my taste, it makes them more sympathetic. He depicts a very harsh world but without an inexorable naturalism that feels obliged to grind them into the dirt. There are also moments of tenderness and goodness. *Newborn* is highly stylized, powerful fiction.

Shoot the Horses First
Leah Angstman
Kernpunkt, 2023

The title page of this collection of short fiction announces its contents not as stories but as "histories." Most of the sixteen narratives are set in the 19th century, some take place even earlier, and the volume includes historical notes and a glossary of Wôpanâak terms. That said, however you want to label them, these texts operate solidly within the conventions literary realism. At their best, they bring to life characters and events that in other accounts are reduced to the dry status of "information" or simply overlooked.

In "The Orphan Train," a Brooklyn boy named Arthur is tossed on a train taking him west, after being told to told "*take the train or take the chain*." This was one of the era's solutions to the problem of homelessness. "The sweepings of New York's streets would become rural America's problem now." His situation is dire, but Angstman avoids determinism and even allows for a glimmer of hope.

Although these histories contain plague, murder, war veterans with post-traumatic stress, improvised amputations—these are not genteel versions of the past—*Shoot the Horses First* doesn't depend on a miserabilist default setting. The relative lawlessness of frontier becomes an opportunity in "In Name Only," where a desperate and disempowered woman and a homosexual rancher can come to a mutually beneficial understanding. Similarly, "A Lifetime of Fishes" rewrites a woman's captivity narrative.

The question of presentism is inescapable in this kind of writing, and it would be unfair to expect Angstman somehow to "solve" it. For better or worse, we cannot escape the perspectives of our era. But the in-the-moment appeal of watching a well-told story unfold is its own reward.

And some of the shorter pieces—"flash histories" in effect—largely avoid the question. "One Night, When the Breath of August Blew Hotter," is a fleeting anecdote of burying a murdered victim. It is strong on imagery but doesn't bother to explain questions of when and why. It is effectively unsettling. Or, in "In the Blood," a quack doctor experiments with transfusing dog blood into humans. (Why not give it a try and see what happens?) In this example, too, brevity without context gives the story added punch.

Wide-ranging and ambitious, *Shoot the Horses First* testifies to the driving force of fiction: curiosity.

She Calls Me Cinnamon
Lane Chasek
Pski's Porch, 2023

In this funny first novel, a young man named Cliff finds himself transformed into a cocker spaniel puppy. Echoes of Gregor Samsa, to be sure, but with a twist: he is convinced that his predicament is because his former human self was murdered, and his new canine identity is a reincarnation. He knows neither the exact cause of his death nor the culprit. So he sets out, like a bewildered four-legged detective, to solve the mystery.

Cliff lives in the care of his ex-girlfriend Phoebe, who calls him Cinnamon. He can still understand human speech but he cannot talk back, and he worries that he is forgetting his human past. He also manages to communicate with other creatures with varying degrees of success. One of them, a pug, turns out to be Father Dvorak, his former priest, who seems rather contented in his new life. Nowadays he's a "fat puddle" more interested in lying in the sun and sleeping than in talking about metempsychosis. Cliff is also pestered by a nitwit raven. Adjusting to this situation is a challenge.

> I have no ability to object or consent to anything, I'm powerless, and the best I can hope for in this new life is getting petted and coddled (which is sometimes nice, but not nice enough).

The book is structured around reminiscences of his past life, in which Cliff worked at a Shell station which he was proud of keeping very clean. His supervisor Oshun is full of opinions about mythology and superheroes and critical exegesis of Fat Albert and the Cosby Kids. In another set piece, he offers a probing stylistic analysis of the comic strip Dilbert. Cliff also recounts his relationship with his autistic sister, Margaret, and sexual shenanigans of his terminally ill mother. Pedophilic predators also figure in the mix. These anecdotes are often darkly amusing but Chasek doesn't settle for the merely whimsical, as there is real pain here.

The ending left me somewhat perplexed by a shift in tone but on the whole, *She Calls Me Cinnamon* is much more than a shaggy dog story. Original and intriguing, the novel mixes elements of the fantastic with acerbic social commentary and an irreverent wit.

Vian, Everett, Theroux

Vercoquin and the Plankton
Boris Vian (tr. Terry Bradford)
Wakefield Press, November 2022

Written in the same fertile half-decade as Vian's two classics—the notorious *I Spit on Your Graves* and the glorious *Froth on the Daydream* a.k.a *Mood Indigo* a.k.a *Foam of the Days*—this long-untranslated novel is a variation on the surreal wonderment of the latter, a less appetising variant of Vianic va-va-voom and bippety-bippety-bop and sca-sca-sca-sca-scat. Anyone who has seen Michel Gondry's sublime adaptation of *Mood Indigo* with Audrey Tautou and Romain Duris—a little slice of cinematic heaven that perfectly captures the effervescent lunacy of Vian's vision—will identify the same youthful flipness and witty malarkey (including sentient mackintoshes) in this recent addition to the English canon from Terry Bradford.

Vercoquin was written along side Vian's first novel *Trouble dans les andains* in 1942-1943, and both remained unpublished until 1966, seven years after his death. In the similar spirit of his other works, as Bradford observes, the novel may be read as a "social documentary, a scathing satire, and a jazz manifesto," and the cryptic punnage and boundless silliness led many critics to dismiss the novel as juvenilia. Vian's early works have that childlike impishness and awe-struck reverence for the possibility of language to create mischief, conjure up roaring gales of laughter, and to traverse the vast unexplored tundras of the imagination, common across his whole short canon, which is all anyone expects from this cheeky master.

Dr. No
Percival Everett
Greywolf Press, November 2022

In Everett's riotous return to comedy following the harrowing heights of *Telephone* and the brutal satire of *The Trees*, America's most prolific and multifaceted novelist serves up a tremendous riff on the realm of Fleming. Wala Kitu (Tagalog words for nothing) is a lecturer on nothing—a svengali of nihil who stimulates his students with wild musings on zip, nada, and zilch—whose non-expertise is purchased by self-styled supervillain John Sill who intends to have his revenge on the America that took him less than seriously. His sidekick is Eigen Vector, a mathematician caught in the spell of Sill whose flip evilness provides the strongest and most violent laughs.

Everett's commitment to sending up the tropes of Bond extends far beyond trapdoors to shark-infested pools (although there is one here), but into a far wittier realm of wordplays about nothing its (non)-self and the mathematical and philosophical contexts of nix, nil, and nowt in relation to our own lives of no significance. Kitu is an inverted Bond—an asexual academic on the autism spectrum who has never driven a car or touched a woman and has a close relationship with his canine Trigo—and is a far more charming presence than the superannuated cliché of vintage Bond movies this novel sends up with sneering vim. Everett is a master of the comedic novel—one that actually elicits a real riptide of LOLs in the reader, not the smirking and oh-so-droll sort found everywhere else—making *Dr. No* an excellent primer for the curious or those seeking the much-needed salve of hilarity in these terminally unfunny times.

Early Stories
Alexander Theroux
Tough Poets Press, August 2021

Fables
Alexander Theroux
Tough Poets Press, December 2021

Slowly treacling into print after half a century, Theroux's short stories are finally available to all long-suffering Therouvians in three lavish volumes (*Later Stories* review coming soon) from Tough Poets Press. In the first volume, Theroux serves up a series of character studies à la 'A Woman with Sauce', a caustic takedown of a doughy harridan fiercely protective of her secret pasta sauce recipe. Other stories are spun from the writer's travels, capturing quirks of dialect and mannerisms, such as 'Fark Pooks', where pornographic magazines are covertly smuggled into the room of a minister by an impish Moscovian porter, 'An English Railroad', where an interminable English pub bore feverishly addled with nostalgia is perfectly parodied, as are the Old World pretensions of a Grande Dame of letters in 'A Wordstress in Williamsburg'. Elsewhere, 'Summer Bellerophon' furthers the theme of nymphet lust explored in *Darconville's Cat*, and 'Chosen Locksley Swims the Tiber' paints a rather dewy-eyed portrait of beauty within a broadly comic poke at the fashion industry. Less successful stories here are the misfires 'Scugnizzo's Pasta Co' and 'The Copernicus Affair', where the mockery spins queasily close to overt racism, or the humour is merely frozen in the period in which the stories were written. Theroux's prose, sentence-by-sentence is among the most stylishly tantalising and exquisite in the American canon, punching up there with Gass and Nabokov in terms of sheer readerly ecstasy, and this collection is an essential read for anyone who wants to be lifted aloft on wings of heavenly prose mastery and led lovingly into rib-tickling comic vistas in the spirit of Fielding and Dickens.

Similarly, a mere twenty-seven years after Dalkey Archive shelved their plans to publish Theroux's *Fables*, the collection is finally available from the unstoppable Tough Poets—among the finest unburyers of lost classics active today. Opening with the fables previously published in illustrated volumes such as 'The Great Wheadle Tragedy'—short fancies of doggerel less charming when stripped of their artistic accompaniment—the volume travels mainly to Europe for a series of character studies similarly rich in accumulated detail and Jamesian perceptivity as those in *Early Stories*. The novella 'The Curse of the White Cartonnage' sees two scheming antique hunters seeking to snaffle precious cartonnage (ancient Egyptian material made from papyrus or linen) from newly arrived neighbours, with invariably parlous consequences. One recurring feature in these stories is Theroux's love for trivia, ribboning every story with a blizzard of knowledge woven into the tapestry of the characters' histories, a technique that occasionally detracts from the story (Theroux has published umpteen books of trivia) but makes for a truly encyclopaedic and incredibly rich reading adventure in the manner of the sexiest Victorian prolixers. The volume also features several fantastical poems in the fable mould.

Mike Silverton

Two Poems

For a Funny Man

You are a funny man.
You look like my underwear
or a bale of cotton with eyes
or shit on my shirt
or he who scurries about with my fingers
or the actor who offers nothing
or a flashy rabbi with a sore throat
or a sagging wall
or the girl who broke my nose
or the man who sits on my arm
or the man who waves goodbye to children
or a bundle of earth
or a game leg
or the Kremlin
or the stool which, if it could walk,
would limp.

(October 30, 1968)

Gnocchi

A planet beset by feet: this is a problem.
On a more intimate scale, why mine? Why yours?
As a poet I'm driven to address difficult issues.
I'm further obliged to mention diaphanous vessels
with mist-like cracks in their unlikely futures.
Though I know I shouldn't, I also dream about you,
even when your cleverest thoughts sound like a bonobo
trying to pronounce gnocchi.

(January 30, 2023)

Contributors

Shahd Alshammari is a Kuwaiti-Palestinian author and academic. She is the author of *Notes on the Flesh* (Faraxa Press, 2017) and *Head Above Water* (Neem Tree Press, 2022).

Polly Atkin is a multi-award-winning writer, essayist and poet based in Grasmere, Cumbria. Her first non-fiction book, *Recovering Dorothy* (2021), will be followed by a memoir in essays exploring place, belonging and chronic illness, *Some of Us Just Fall* (July, 2023).

Greg Bem is a poet and librarian in Seattle.

Jesi Bender is an artist from Upstate New York. She helms KERNPUNKT Press, a home for experimental writing. She is the author of *Dangerous Women* (dancing girl press, 2022), *Kinderkrankenhaus* (Sagging Meniscus, 2021), and *The Book of the Last Word* (Whiskey Tit, 2019). She reviews books under the name **Jesi Buell**.

P.J. Blumenthal, an American writer in Munich, Germany, writes in both German and English. He is the author of a non-fiction book on feral man, *Kaspar Hausers Geschwister* (Kaspar Hauser's Siblings), and a German-language blog, "Der Sprachbloggeur."

Deaf Irish author **Lynn Buckle,** judge and former winner of the international Barbellion Prize for chronically ill and disabled published authors, is widely published. She represented Ireland as a UNESCO City of Literature Writer in Residence at the National Centre for Writing UK 2021 and hosts the worldwide Climate Writers at the Irish Writers Centre, Dublin.

Marvin Cohen is the author of many novels, plays, and collections of essays, stories, and poems. He lives on the Lower East Side of Manhattan.

Michael Collins is the author of four collections of poetry, most recently *Appearances*. He teaches at NYU and the Hudson Valley Writers' Center and is the Poet Laureate of Mamaroneck, NY.

Mark DuCharme is the author of *We, the Monstrous: Script for an Unrealizable Film*, *Counter Fluencies 1-20*, *The Unfinished: Books I-VI*, *Answer*, *The Sensory Cabinet* and other works. *Scorpion Letters* will be published as a chapbook by Ethel in 2022. A recipient of the Neodata Endowment in Literature and the Gertrude Stein Award in Innovative American Poetry, he lives in Boulder, Colorado.

William Erickson is a poet and memoirist from the Southwest of Washington State. His chapbook, *Monotonies of the Wildlife*, is out February 2022 (FLP).

Jack Foley's numerous books of poetry, fiction and criticism include *Visions and Affiliations*, a "chronoencyclopedia" of California poetry from 1940 to 2005, *Grief Songs* (SM, 2017) and *When Sleep Comes* (SM, 2020). He lives in Oakland and hosts a weekly radio show, *Cover to Cover*, on Berkeley's Pacifica station, KPFA.

Lauren Foley (she/her) is Irish/Australian and a Next Generation Artist in Literature with the Arts Council of Ireland. Bisexual, chronically ill and disabled, she has a plethora of health issues including: Lupus (SLE), endometriosis and mental illness, and the majority of her writing is dictated. Lauren won the inaugural Overland Neilma Sidney Short Story Prize and The Los Angeles Review, Creative Nonfiction Award. Her work has been shortlisted for the Irish Book Awards and is published in the critically acclaimed *The Art of the Glimpse: 100 Irish Short Stories* selected by Sinéad Gleeson.

Cal Freeman is the author of the books *Fight Songs* (2017) and *Poolside at the Dearborn Inn* (forthcoming from R&R Press in April 2022). He currently serves as Writer-In-Residence with InsideOut Literary Arts Detroit and teaches at Oakland University.

Jason Graff's debut novel *Stray Our Pieces*, published in the fall of 2019, concerns a woman extricating herself from motherhood. In early 2020, *heckler*, about lives colliding at a struggling hotel, was released by Unsolicited Press. He lives in Plano, TX with his wife and their son.

John Patrick Higgins is a playwright, short story writer, screenwriter and director. He lives in Belfast.

Tomoé Hill's work has appeared in such publications as *Socrates on the Beach*, *The London Magazine*, *Vol. 1 Brooklyn*, *3:AM Magazine*, *Music & Literature*, *Numéro Cinq*, and *Lapsus Lima*, as well as the anthologies *We'll Never Have Paris* (Repeater Books), *Azimuth* (Sonic Art Research Unit at Oxford Brookes University), and *Trauma: Essays on Art and Mental Health* (Dodo Ink). Her *Songs of Olympia*, essays in response to Michel Leiris' *The Ribbon at Olympia's Throat*, is forthcoming from Sagging Meniscus in 2023.

Charles Holdefer is an American writer currently based in Brussels. His stories have appeared in the *New England Review*, *Chicago Quarterly Review* and *Slice*. His latest book is *Don't Look at Me* (SM, 2022).

David Holzman is a concert pianist who has won acclaim for his performances and recordings of many of the 20th Century's most challenging masterpieces. His essay on pianism, specific composers and himself have appeared in numerous scholarly journals and he has appeared in numerous films. He is Professor at Long Island University.

Tom La Farge (1947 –2020) was a novelist, educator, and publisher who lived in Brooklyn, New York. He was the author of more than a dozen books, including *The Crimson Bears* (Sun & Moon Press), *Zuntig* (Green Integer), and *The Enchantments Trilogy* (Spuyten Duyvil), and was the editor of Proteotypes, a small press based in Brooklyn. To learn more about Tom and the award that now bears his name, please see:thetomlafargeaward.com.

Kurt Luchs is the author of *Falling in the Direction of Up* (SM, 2020), *One of These Things Is Not Like the Other* (Finishing Line Press, 2019), and the humor collection *It's Funny Until Someone Loses an Eye (Then It's* Really *Funny)* (SM, 2017). He lives in Michigan.

Melissa McCarthy's *Sharks, Death, Surfers: An Illustrated Companion* was published by Sternberg in 2019. Her next book, *Photo, Phyto, Proto, Nitro*, comes out with SM in the autumn of 2023. In the meantime, other pieces from *Full Stop* magazine, *Public Domain Review*, *The Yellow Paper*, and more; and her two radio series—Melissa McCarthy's *View from a Shark* and *The Slipping Forecast*—can be found at sharksillustrated.org. She lives in Edinburgh.

Malcolm McCollum is a prominent Colorado ne'er-do-well.

Letty McHugh is an artist and writer based in West Yorkshire.

R.S. Mengert's work has appeared in *Pensive,SurVision, Zymbol, Poor Yorick, Maintenant, Poetry is Dead, ABZ, Four Chambers, The Café Review, Fjords, San Pedro River Review*, and *Enizagam*. He lives in Tempe,AZ, with his wife and an unusually loud cat.

Jefferson Navicky is the author of *Antique Densities*, a book of modern parables, as well as the novella, *The Book of Transparencies*, and the story collection, *The Paper Coast*. He works as the archivist for the Maine Women Writers Collection, and lives on the coast of Maine.

Kathleen Nicholls is an author and illustrator, best known for *Go Your Crohn Way*, the first of three books loosely based on her own experiences with chronic illness. She lives and works in central Scotland.

M.J. Nicholls' most recent novel is *Condemned to Cymru* (SM, 2022). He lives in Glasgow.

Dan O'Brien is a poet, playwright, and essayist. Acre Books published his fourth poetry collection, *Our Cancers*, in 2021, and will publish a collection of his prose poems, *Survivor's Notebook*, later this year. He lives in Los Angeles.

Harry Parker is the author of *Anatomy of a Soldier* (2016), translated in eight languages. He grew up in Wiltshire, and was educated at Falmouth College of Art and University College London. He joined the British Army when he was 23 and served in Iraq in 2007 and Afghanistan in 2009 as a Captain. He is now a writer and artist and lives in London.

Elizabeth Robinson is the author of *Being Modernist Together*, forthcoming from Solid Objects in 2022. Recent work has appeared in, or is slated to appear in *Big Other, Conjunctions, Fence, New Letters, Plume*, and *Volt*.

David Rose, born 1949, resident in Britain, is now retired after a working life in the Post Office. His short stories are published widely in the UK and US, including in *The Penguin Book of the Contemporary Short Story* (ed. Philip Hensher, 2018) and partly collected in *Posthumous Stories* (Salt, 2013). He is the author of two novels: *Vault* (Salt, 2011) and *Meridian* (Unthank Books, 2015).

Tom Shakespeare is a British academic, writer and broadcaster. His first novel, *The Ha-ha*, will be published by Farrago in 2024.

Mike Silverton's poetry appeared in the late 60s and early 70s in *Harper's*, *The Nation*, and many other publications. He is the author of *Trios* (SM, 2023) and *Anvil on a Shoestring* (SM, 2022).

Doug Smith has trained hospice workers in all fifty US states. He is now now taking patient stories and putting them into fictional form.

Will Stanier currently lives in Tucson where he is training to be a librarian. He is the author of a chapbook, *Everything Happens Next* (Blue Arrangements, 2021).

Matthew Tomkinson is a writer, composer, and researcher. He holds a PhD in Theatre Studies from the University of British Columbia, where he studied sound within the Deaf, Disability, and Mad arts. He is the author of *oems* (Guernica Editions, 2022), *Paroxysms* (Paper View Books, 2022), *For a Long Time* (Frog Hollow Press, 2019), and *Archaic Torso of Gumby* (Gordon Hill Press, 2020), co-authored with Geoffrey D. Morrison.

Dan Tremaglio's stories have appeared in various publications, including *F(r)iction*, *Gravel*, *Literary Orphans*, and *Flash Fiction Magazine*, and twice been named a finalist for the Calvino Prize. He teaches creative writing and literature at Bellevue College outside Seattle where he is a senior editor for the journal *Belletrist*.

Thomas Walton is the author of *Good Morning Bone Crusher*! (Spuyten Duyvil, 2021), *All the Useless Things Are Mine* (SM, 2020), *The World Is All That Does Befall Us* (Ravenna Press, 2019), and *The Last Mosaic* (with Elizabeth Cooperman, SM, 2018). He lives in Seattle, WA.